For more than 50 years, *The Australian Women's Weekly* Test Kitchen has been creating marvellous recipes that come with a guarantee of success. First, the recipes always work – just follow the instructions and you too will get the results you see in the photographs. Second, and perhaps more importantly, they are delicious – created by experienced home economists and chefs, all triple-tested and, thanks to their straightforward instructions, easy to make.

British and North American readers:
Please note that Australian cup and spoon measurements are metric.
A quick conversion guide appears on page 119.

If there were any question that we are indeed a lucky country, a visit to the many growers and produce markets across Australia would set the record straight. Our parents may have had to make do with meat and three veg, but today we are spoiled for choice with a variety, quality and freshness we have come to take for granted. We have multiculturalism to thank for the diversity of our cuisine, our primary producers for their dedication to quality and our cooks for their boundless enthusiasm and endless innovation. We hope you enjoy the fruits of their combined labours, presented in the same easy, relaxed style with which Australians like to entertain.

Pamela Clark

FOOD EDITOR

contents

EASY AUSTRALIAN STYLE

eating australian style
ALL YEAR ROUND

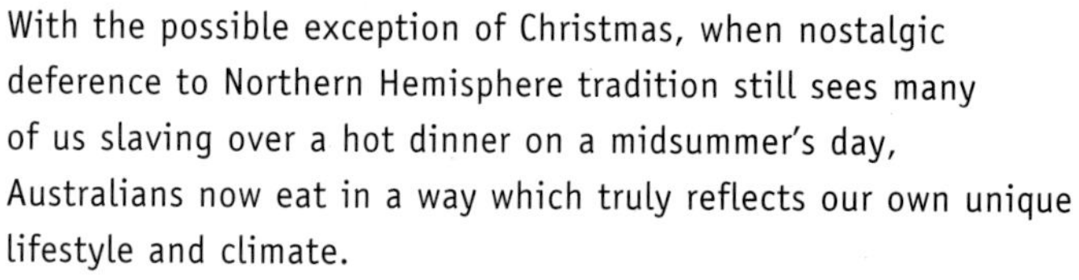

AUSTRALIAN HORTICULTURAL CORPORATION

PETER SOLNESS

DARLING HARBOUR AUTHORITY

With the possible exception of Christmas, when nostalgic deference to Northern Hemisphere tradition still sees many of us slaving over a hot dinner on a midsummer's day, Australians now eat in a way which truly reflects our own unique lifestyle and climate.

Growing in a haphazard way from an inauspicious start — salted meat, weevil-ridden flour and vegetables that refused to thrive — the development of Australian food has been more a matter of what was available and what would grow than a conscious attempt at creating an identifiable cuisine. Of course, if the first settlers had only recognised it, they were surrounded by bountiful provision of every kind, native food that had sustained the indigenous people of Australia for thousands of years before white settlement.

The absence of a specific "national cuisine" has meant that we have been free to borrow and adapt whatever suited and attracted us from other cultures. Augmented at intervals by the arrival of various ethnic groups — the Chinese during the 19th century gold rushes, Europeans after World War II and South-East Asian refugees following wars in Vietnam and Cambodia — the population of Australia has seen culinary tastes change dramatically over 200 years. The result today is a delightfully eclectic mix of Mediterranean and Asian influences that exist side by side with aspects of a cuisine inherited from our colonial forebears. Take, for instance, that most traditional of Australian meals, a roast leg of lamb. Once always served with baked vegetables, peas and mint sauce, it is just as likely these days to be spiked with rosemary and garlic and slow-roasted in the Greek fashion, or rubbed with spices and yogurt and cooked over glowing coals in an Australian version of tandoori.

The sheer size of Australia means that seasonality scarcely exists — as the season for a particular fruit finishes in one state, that same fruit is beginning to ripen in another part of the country so we are rarely without. This availability and diversity have resulted in an emphasis on fresh ingredients and a simple style of preparation that relies on that very freshness for its effect — if produce is good enough in the first place, why gild the lily?

SCOTT CAMERON

DARLING HARBOUR AUTHORITY

It is something of a cliché that Australia is an outdoor nation, but nonetheless true. When much of the country enjoys warm, sunny conditions for at least part of the year, the love of the outdoors is understandable and meals outside play an important part in our lifestyle, whether it's a barbecue with family and friends in the back yard, an alfresco meal at a restaurant, a picnic in the bush, a pie at the football, or fish and chips on the beach.

This book is a celebration of all the things that have come to characterise Australian food today — an emphasis on the freshest ingredients from an unpolluted environment, a variety of culinary influences from all over the world, simple, unpretentious methods of preparation, and a willingness to experiment and embrace the new while cherishing the best of the past.

HAMILTON LUND ATC

starters

the freshest ingredients are the secret to these enticing first courses

rolled sushi

preparation time 30 minutes (plus refrigeration time) ■ cooking time 20 minutes

You can substitute white, medium-grain rice such as calrose if koshihikari rice is hard to find. Nowadays, large supermarkets often sell Japanese ingredients, such as the tissue-thin seaweed sheets called nori, used for wrapping sushi, as well as sichimi togarashi, a mixture of ground spices, also called Japanese pepper.

2 cups (400g) koshihikari rice
3 cups (750ml) boiling water
2 tablespoons rice vinegar
1 tablespoon sugar
1 teaspoon salt
2 teaspoons peanut oil
2 eggs, beaten lightly
1/4 cup (35g) black sesame seeds
2 sheets toasted nori
1 tablespoon wasabi
1 small red capsicum (150g), sliced thinly
1 Lebanese cucumber (130g), seeded, sliced thinly
1 small carrot (70g), sliced thinly
1 tablespoon Japanese pepper

1. Place rice in large saucepan with the boiling water; simmer, covered, about 15 minutes or until tender, stirring occasionally. Stir in vinegar, sugar and salt; spread rice in single layer on large tray. Refrigerate until cold.
2. Heat half the oil in wok or large non-stick frying pan. Add half the egg, swirl wok so egg forms a thin omelette over base; cook until set, remove, cool. Repeat with remaining oil and egg. Roll omelettes firmly; slice thinly.
3. Sprinkle one-quarter of the sesame seeds on a plastic-wrap-lined bamboo sushi mat. Using wet fingers, pat one-quarter of the rice mixture over seeds. Halve nori sheets; place 1 piece nori on rice. On the narrow side closest to you, spread one-quarter of the wasabi in a thin line along edge of nori; cover wasabi with one-quarter each of the capsicum, cucumber, carrot and egg strips. Using narrow side of mat closest to you, start rolling sushi, pressing firmly as you roll. Cut roll into six pieces; sprinkle with pepper. Repeat process with remaining ingredients to make a total of four rolls; you will have 24 pieces of rolled sushi.

SERVES 8

per serving 5.4g fat; 1058kJ

tip Serve rolls with separate small bowls of soy sauce, pickled ginger slices and extra wasabi.

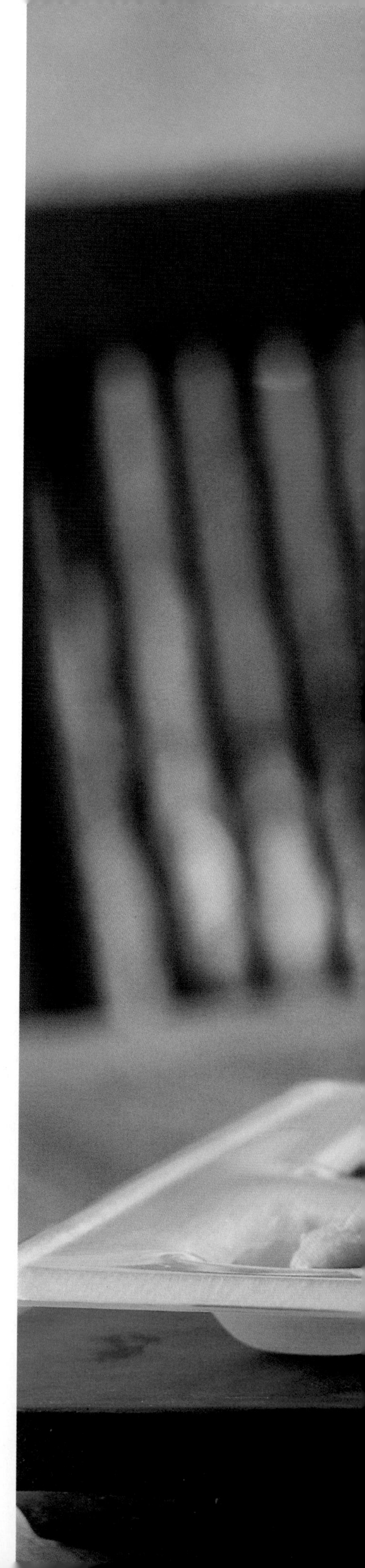

herbed baked *ricotta* with chilli oil and *bruschetta*

preparation time 20 minutes ■ cooking time 1 hour

Dense, crusty, wood-fired bread such as ciabatta is essential to the success of the grilled bread known as bruschetta,which translates from the Italian as "roughly or abruptly cut".

1kg fresh ricotta cheese
2 tablespoons finely chopped fresh lemon thyme
2 cloves garlic, crushed
2 eggs, beaten lightly
1 tablespoon finely chopped garlic chives
2 red Thai chillies, seeded, chopped finely
1 tablespoon finely grated lemon rind
½ loaf ciabatta (275g), sliced thinly
2 tablespoons olive oil
50g baby rocket leaves
½ cup (125ml) chilli oil

1. Press cheese into colander, place over large bowl to drain; cover cheese with inverted saucer, weigh down with heavy can. Refrigerate overnight.
2. Preheat oven to moderate. Grease 20cm-round deep cake pan; line base with baking paper.
3. Place drained cheese in large bowl with thyme, garlic, egg, chives, chilli and rind; stir until well combined. Spoon cheese mixture into prepared pan; bake, uncovered, in moderate oven about 1 hour or until browned lightly and firm to the touch. Cool in pan.
4. Meanwhile, brush ciabatta slices both sides with olive oil; toast both sides under hot grill.
5. Serve cheese in wedges with rocket and bruschetta; drizzle with chilli oil.

SERVES 8

per serving 35.7g fat; 1943kJ

tip While fresh ricotta cheese has a short life, once baked it will keep, covered, in the refrigerator for up to three days. Try adding a few tablespoons of finely chopped pancetta or black olives to ricotta mixture before baking.

goat-cheese-stuffed *roast capsicum* with tapenade

preparation time 30 minutes ■ cooking time 20 minutes (plus standing time)

The name tapenade derives from tapeno, the Provençal word for capers, a vital ingredient in this tangy condiment that perfectly complements goat cheese. The first olives were brought to South Australia from Marseilles in 1844 and that state now boasts a number of commercial growing areas, although demand outstrips local supply so most olive oil is still imported.

4 medium red capsicums (800g)
300g firm goat cheese
200g fresh ricotta cheese
2 tablespoons sour cream
2 tablespoons extra virgin olive oil
1 tablespoon basil leaves
cracked black pepper

TAPENADE

1 tablespoon drained capers
3 anchovy fillets, drained
1/2 cup seeded black olives (60g)
1 tablespoon lemon juice
1/4 cup (60ml) extra virgin olive oil

1. Roast whole capsicums under grill or in very hot oven until skin blisters and blackens. Cover capsicum with plastic or paper for 5 minutes; peel away skin. Slice off and discard top and bottom of capsicums; carefully remove and discard seeds and membrane from inside remaining capsicum pieces. Trim capsicum pieces to 8cm in depth; cut each in half to make two 4cm "rings" (you will have eight rings).
2. Blend or process cheeses and sour cream until smooth. Fit one capsicum ring inside a 5.5cm-round cutter, place on serving plate, spoon cheese mixture inside capsicum ring; carefully remove cutter. Repeat with remaining capsicum and cheese mixture.
3. Serve capsicum with tapenade, drizzle with oil, sprinkle with basil leaves and cracked pepper.

Tapenade Blend or process ingredients until smooth.

SERVES 8

per serving 30g fat; 1412kJ

oysters with green onion dressing

preparation time 10 minutes

24 oysters, on the half shell
rock salt

GREEN ONION DRESSING
2 green onions, chopped finely
1 red Thai chilli, seeded, chopped finely
2 tablespoons finely chopped fresh coriander leaves
1/2 small Lebanese cucumber (65g), seeded, chopped finely
1 clove garlic, crushed
2 tablespoons lime juice
1/2 cup (125ml) peanut oil

1. Remove oysters from shells; reserve shells. Drain oysters on absorbent paper. Wash and dry reserved shells; return oysters to shells.
2. Serve oysters on bed of rock salt; top with green onion dressing.

green onion dressing Combine ingredients in small bowl.

SERVES 4

per serving 30.6g fat; 1231kJ
tip Oysters can also be served on a bed of crushed ice.

oysters with bloody mary granita and vodka shots

preparation time 15 minutes (plus freezing time)
cooking time 10 minutes

Granita is an Italian ice confection, made here with the ingredients of a Bloody Mary cocktail and served with a shot glass of vodka on the side.

1/4 cup (55g) caster sugar
1/4 cup (60ml) water
1 1/2 cups (375ml) tomato juice
2 tablespoons lemon juice
2 teaspoons Tabasco sauce
2 teaspoons Worcestershire sauce
24 oysters, on the half shell
8 x 30ml shots vodka, to serve

1. Combine sugar and the water in small saucepan; stir over heat, without boiling, until sugar dissolves. Remove from heat.
2. Stir both juices and both sauces into sugar syrup; pour into 14cm x 21cm loaf pan, cover with foil; freeze about 3 hours or until firm.
3. Remove oysters from shells; reserve shells. Drain oysters on absorbent paper. Wash and dry reserved shells; return oysters to shells.
4. Just before serving, top oysters with small scoops of granita; serve with vodka shots.

SERVES 8

per serving 0.5g fat; 360kJ
tip You can serve the oysters on a bed of crushed ice and the granita separately in small wine glasses. A shot, also known as a jigger, measures 30ml.

Sydney rock oysters are farmed along the eastern coast of Australia. They have a thick, crinkly shell and creamy-golden flesh. Although the larger Pacific and native flat oysters are also grown in Australia, many enthusiasts argue that the Sydney rock oyster has no peer.

zucchini flowers filled with suppli *rice*

preparation time 20 minutes ■ cooking time 45 minutes

Zucchini flowers are one of summer's fleeting delights and during their brief season, if you're not fortunate enough to grow your own, they can sometimes be a lucky find at your greengrocer's. Buy them if you get the opportuntity and fill them with this mixture of rice, fetta and parmesan, inspired by the Italian croquettes known as suppli.

2 teaspoons olive oil
1 small brown onion (80g), chopped finely
1 clove garlic, crushed
1/2 cup (100g) arborio rice
1/4 cup (60ml) dry white wine
1 1/2 cups (375ml) chicken stock
1/4 cup (20g) finely grated parmesan cheese
50g fetta cheese, chopped coarsely
18 fresh zucchini flowers (approximately 250g)
150g baby spinach leaves
1/3 cup loosely packed fresh basil leaves
1/3 cup loosely packed fresh flat-leaf parsley
1 tablespoon balsamic vinegar
2 tablespoons olive oil, extra
2/3 cup (50g) parmesan cheese, shaved

1 Heat oil in medium saucepan; cook onion and garlic, stirring, until onion is soft. Add rice, wine and stock, bring to a boil; simmer, uncovered, stirring occasionally, about 12 minutes or until rice is tender and liquid is absorbed. Stir in grated parmesan and fetta; cool.

2 Preheat oven to very hot. Remove and discard stamens from centre of zucchini flowers; fill flowers with rice mixture, twist petal tops to enclose filling. Place filled flowers on oiled oven tray; roast, uncovered, in very hot oven about 15 minutes or until browned lightly and heated through.

3 Meanwhile, combine spinach, basil and parsley in medium bowl, toss with combined vinegar and extra oil. Serve zucchini flowers with spinach salad; sprinkle with shaved cheese.

SERVES 6

per serving 12.4g fat; 902kJ

tip We used fetta cheese in the filling, but you can substitute mozzarella or fontina, if you prefer.

kumara *gnocchi* with sage burnt butter

preparation time 1 hour (plus refrigeration time) ■ cooking time 10 minutes

The secret of perfect gnocchi, these melt-in-the-mouth Italian dumplings, is light handling and little cooking. As soon as the gnocchi float to the surface of the boiling water, they are ready. You can substitute white sweet potato, if you wish, but you will sacrifice the rich orange colour of the kumara.

200g kumara, peeled, chopped coarsely
1 tablespoon olive oil
2 medium potatoes (400g), chopped coarsely
2 tablespoons finely grated parmesan cheese
1 teaspoon ground nutmeg
1 clove garlic, crushed
1 teaspoon salt
1 egg, beaten lightly
1 cup (150g) plain flour
2/3 cup (50g) parmesan cheese, shaved

SAGE BURNT BUTTER
150g butter
2 tablespoons finely chopped fresh sage leaves

1 Preheat oven to hot.
2 Place kumara in small baking dish, drizzle with oil; bake, uncovered, in hot oven about 30 minutes or until kumara is tender. Trim any blackened edges.
3 Meanwhile, boil, steam or microwave potato until tender; drain.
4 Mash kumara and potato together in large bowl until smooth; stir in cheese, nutmeg, garlic, salt and egg. Using hands, mix in flour. Turn dough onto floured surface; knead lightly about 2 minutes or until smooth. Roll heaped teaspoons of mixture into gnocchi-shaped ovals; press lightly against back of fork tines. Place gnocchi on tray, cover; refrigerate 30 minutes.
5 Cook gnocchi in large saucepan of boiling water, uncovered, about 10 minutes or until gnocchi float to surface. Remove gnocchi from pan with slotted spoon; drain.
6 Serve gnocchi tossed with sage burnt butter; top with flaked cheese.

sage burnt butter While gnocchi are cooking, melt butter in medium frying pan; cook until butter turns nut-brown in colour, stir in sage.

SERVES 6

per serving 28.4g fat; 1760kJ

seared *atlantic salmon* with dill and asparagus

preparation time 15 minutes ■ cooking time 30 minutes

SALAMANCA MARKETS, HOBART, TASMANIA
Joe Shemesh ATC

80g angel-hair pasta
400g piece Atlantic salmon
1 tablespoon olive oil
500g asparagus, trimmed, chopped coarsely
20g butter
1 clove garlic, crushed
1 teaspoon seeded mustard
1 teaspoon Dijon mustard
1 tablespoon finely shredded lemon rind
2 tablespoons lemon juice
½ cup (125ml) chicken stock
100ml crème fraîche
¼ cup coarsely chopped fresh dill
3 green onions, sliced thinly

1. Cook pasta in large saucepan of boiling water, uncovered, until just tender; drain, keep warm.
2. Meanwhile, cut salmon into 2cm cubes.
3. Heat half the oil in large non-stick frying pan; cook asparagus over high heat, turning, until browned slightly and just tender. Drain on absorbent paper.
4. Heat remaining oil in same pan; cook salmon over high heat, turning, until just seared. Drain on absorbent paper.
5. Melt butter in same pan; cook garlic, stirring, until fragrant. Add mustards, rind, juice and stock, bring to a boil. Stir in crème fraîche, dill and onion; heat without boiling. Add pasta, asparagus and salmon; toss gently to combine.

SERVES 4

per serving 20.5g fat; 1474kJ

tip This dish can also be served as a light lunch. Light sour cream can be used to replace crème fraîche, which is a cultured cream product made by combining buttermilk or sour cream with pure cream. You could also substitute tarragon and patty pan squash for dill and asparagus. We used angel-hair, a fine, long pasta, in this recipe, but you can use any long pasta.

Some of the best Atlantic salmon in the world is farmed off the coast of Tasmania. Here, it is lightly seared to preserve its delicate fresh flavour and served with angel-hair pasta and crisp, fresh stalks of locally grown asparagus, at its best during spring and summer.

the salty taste of the sea

SYDNEY ROCK OYSTERS

One of the simplest of life's pleasures must surely be a plate of freshly shucked Sydney rock oysters and lots of slices of brown bread and butter. If you can watch the ocean while you enjoy this feast, so much the better.

The name Sydney rock oyster is something of a misnomer as it seems to imply that the oysters are found only around the Sydney region. In fact, they grow naturally along a considerable part of the eastern Australian coastline, from Wingan Inlet in Victoria to Moreton Bay in Queensland, and are also farmed in Tasmania, South Australia and Western Australia. The "Sydney" tag is also a rather modern appellation, since by the time Captain Phillip arrived in Sydney Harbour in 1788 and gave it that name, the Aboriginal population of the eastern seaboard had been harvesting the native oysters for thousands of years.

Commercial cultivation of Sydney rock oysters began around 1870. Unlike the wholly farmed oysters of the other states, the New South Wales oysters are generally grown from tiny wild hatchlings known as spat that are produced by the natural colonies of rock oysters along the coast. These spat attach themselves to sticks that are then placed in racks in the tidal waters of estuaries. Alternatively, the spat are removed from the sticks and placed on trays which are suspended in the water. This latter method, known as singleseed, is thought to lead to a better shape and quality of oyster. It takes about four years for an oyster to develop from a spat into a marketable-sized product.

The flavour of an oyster will depend on its environment: tidal conditions, salinity, drought, flood and rain all have an important effect on the taste. Since oysters live on algae that they filter out of the water, it is vital that the water itself remains fresh and uncontaminated. Since 1997, all oysters grown in New South Wales must be tested by law under a quality assurance program, which aims to maintain a high meat standard and detect any possible contamination before it reaches the market.

oyster bar, sydney harbour AUSTRALIAN TOURIST COMMISSI

sydney harbour, new south wales SCOTT CAMERON

taste-testing sydney rock oysters SCOTT CAMERON

Sydney rock oysters will live out of water and remain in prime condition for up to two weeks if kept out of direct light in cool, moist conditions, such as in a damp hessian bag. When you open an oyster, it should be full of water, the meat should be plump and moist and it should smell of the sea. Freshly shucked oysters will also keep in the refrigerator for up to three days, but why wait?

freshly shucked sydney rock oysters SCOTT CAMERON

poached *egg salad*

preparation time 20 minutes ■ cooking time 10 minutes

The rustic bread, ciabatta, so named in Italy because its shape resembles a slipper, makes a crunchy counterpoint to a mixed leaf salad. Balsamic vinegar is traditionally made from sweet trebbiano grapes and matured in wooden casks.

1/2 loaf ciabatta (275g)
8 slices prosciutto (120g)
2 tablespoons olive oil
4 eggs
100g mesclun
1/4 cup (60ml) olive oil, extra
2 tablespoons balsamic vinegar
1 clove garlic, crushed
1 tablespoon seeded mustard

1 Cut ciabatta into eight thin slices. Cut each slice of prosciutto lengthways into three strips.

2 Heat half the oil in large frying pan; cook bread until browned both sides. Heat remaining oil in same pan; cook prosciutto until browned and crisp, drain on absorbent paper.

3 Poach eggs in large frying pan of barely simmering water until the whites are set but the yolks are still soft.

4 Meanwhile, toss mesclun in large bowl with combined remaining ingredients; divide among serving plates. Drain eggs; top each salad with an egg, serve with ciabatta and prosciutto.

SERVES 4

per serving 34.3g fat; 2189kJ

tip Ensure the water is at a very low simmer before poaching the eggs; you can remove the pan from the heat and stand it, covered, for about 2 minutes until eggs are cooked as desired.

risotto primavera on grilled flat mushrooms

preparation time 20 minutes ■ cooking time 45 minutes

Primavera is Italian for spring, and the freshest of seasonal vegetables are used in this risotto, made traditionally with arborio rice, a wide-grained, pearly variety which readily absorbs stock without becoming mushy.

1 litre (4 cups) chicken stock
1 cup (250ml) dry white wine
20g butter
1 tablespoon olive oil
1 medium brown onion (150g), chopped finely
2 green onions, sliced thinly
1 clove garlic, crushed
1 1/4 cups (250g) arborio rice
250g asparagus, trimmed, sliced thickly
100g snow peas, halved
100g sugar snap peas
2 tablespoons finely chopped fresh chives
1/4 cup (60ml) cream
1/4 cup (20g) finely grated parmesan cheese
4 flat mushrooms (360g)
1 tablespoon finely chopped fresh chives, extra

1 Combine stock and wine in medium saucepan; bring to a boil, then simmer.

2 Meanwhile, heat butter and oil in large saucepan; cook both onions and garlic, stirring, until onion softens. Add rice, stir to coat in oil mixture. Stir in 1 cup of hot stock mixture; cook, stirring, over low heat until liquid is absorbed. Continue adding stock mixture, in 1-cup batches, stirring until absorbed between each addition. Total cooking time should be about 35 minutes or until rice is tender.

3 Gently stir in asparagus, snow peas, sugar snap peas, chives, cream and cheese; stand, covered, 5 minutes.

4 While risotto is standing, cook mushrooms on heated oiled grill plate (or grill or barbecue) until browned and tender.

5 Serve risotto on mushrooms; sprinkle with extra chives.

SERVES 4

per serving 18g fat; 2248kJ

tip Snap the woody ends off the asparagus spears before slicing them.

caramelised *onion* and *brie* tart

preparation time 30 minutes (plus refrigeration time) ■ cooking time 1 hour

KING ISLAND BRIE, TASMANIA
The King Island Company Limited

1 1/4 cups (185g) plain flour
125g cold butter, chopped
2 egg yolks
2 tablespoons iced water
30g butter, extra
2 large brown onions (400g), sliced thinly
2 teaspoons brown sugar
150g ripe brie cheese, chopped coarsely
1/3 cup (80ml) cream
2 eggs, beaten lightly
1/4 teaspoon ground nutmeg
250g rocket leaves
2 tablespoons raspberry vinegar

1. Preheat oven to moderately hot.
2. Process flour and butter until crumbly; add egg yolks and water, process until ingredients just come together. Knead dough gently on floured surface until smooth, cover; refrigerate 30 minutes.
3. Roll pastry between sheets of baking paper until large enough to line 11cm x 35cm rectangular or 23cm-round flan tin. Lift pastry into tin, press into sides, trim edges; place tin on oven tray. Cover pastry with baking paper, fill with dried beans or rice; bake in moderately hot oven about 10 minutes. Remove paper and beans; bake, uncovered, 10 minutes or until browned lightly. Cool pastry case.
4. Melt extra butter in large frying pan; cook onion, stirring, about 15 minutes or until softened. Add sugar; cook, stirring, about 15 minutes or until onion is caramelised. Remove from heat, stir in cheese; allow to cool then spoon into pastry case. Pour over combined cream, egg and nutmeg; bake, uncovered, in moderate oven about 30 minutes or until filling sets and tart is browned lightly. Serve tart with rocket leaves tossed in vinegar.

SERVES 6

per serving 38.3g fat; 2103kJ
tip Pastry case and caramelised onion can be made a day ahead.

Slow cooking in butter and brown sugar produces sweet, caramelised onions that team beautifully with the creamy richness of a perfectly ripe brie to make this simple yet very elegant tart.

aussie *antipasti*

The word antipasto means "before the pasta", but these appetisers could stand alone as a complete meal. Each recipe serves 8.

lavash bread *triangles*

preparation time 5 minutes
cooking time 8 minutes

2 pieces lavash bread

1 Preheat oven to moderate.
2 Cut bread into quarters; halve quarters to form triangles.
3 Place bread on oven trays; bake, uncovered, in moderate oven about 8 minutes or until crisp.

per serving 0.5g fat; 206kJ

tip Try toasting lavash bread whole, then break roughly into shards.

pickled *sardines*

preparation time 10 minutes
(plus overnight marinating)

8 sardine fillets (120g)
1 cup (250ml) lemon juice
2 cloves garlic, crushed
2 tablespoons coarsely chopped fresh flat-leaf parsley

1 Place fish in single layer in shallow dish; pour over combined juice, garlic and parsley. Cover; refrigerate overnight. Drain; discard marinade.

per serving 0.5g fat; 109kJ

kumara and celeriac *chips*

preparation time 15 minutes
cooking time 15 minutes

vegetable oil, for deep-frying
1 medium kumara (400g), sliced thinly
1kg celeriac, trimmed, sliced thinly

1 Heat oil in wok or large saucepan. Deep-fry kumara and celeriac, in batches, until browned and crisp; drain on absorbent paper.

per serving 8.5g fat; 561kJ

tip Other root vegetables or tubers, such as carrot, beetroot or parsnip, can be made into chips.

rocket and prosciutto *frittata*

preparation time 15 minutes
cooking time 35 minutes (plus standing time)

8 slices prosciutto (120g)
40g rocket leaves
2 tablespoons finely grated parmesan cheese
10 eggs, beaten lightly
2 tablespoons cream

1 Preheat oven to moderate.
2 Grease deep 19cm-square cake pan; line base and two opposite sides with baking paper.
3 Cook prosciutto, in batches, in medium non-stick frying pan until browned all over and crisp; drain on absorbent paper.
4 Place half of the prosciutto in prepared pan; cover with half of the rocket then half of the cheese. Repeat with remaining prosciutto, rocket and cheese.
5 Pour combined egg and cream into pan, pressing down on prosciutto mixture to completely cover with egg mixture; bake, uncovered, in moderate oven about 30 minutes or until firm. Stand 5 minutes; turn out of pan, cut into 16 pieces.

per serving 11.3g fat; 626kJ

tip Serve frittata hot or cold.

marinated *olives*

preparation time 10 minutes
(plus marinating time)

250g green olives
250g kalamata olives
2 lime wedges
2 cups (500ml) olive oil (approx)
1 clove garlic, sliced thinly
1/3 cup (80ml) lime juice
6 sprigs fresh thyme, halved
3 sprigs fresh rosemary

1 Combine ingredients in large sterilised jar, ensuring olives are covered in oil; seal jar.

per serving 22.4g fat; 1011kJ

tip Olives are best made at least two weeks before you serve them; store, covered, in a cool dark place.

marinated goat-cheese *fetta*

preparation time 10 minutes
(plus marinating time)

10 black peppercorns
750g goat-cheese fetta, cut into 2cm cubes
5 red Thai chillies, sliced thinly
4 bay leaves
1/4 cup (60ml) lemon juice
3 cups (750ml) olive oil
1 clove garlic, sliced thinly
3 sprigs fresh rosemary
3 sprigs fresh thyme

1 Combine ingredients in sterilised jar, ensuring fetta is covered with oil; seal jar.

per serving 36.7g fat; 1657kJ

tip Fetta can be stored, covered, in a cool dark place up to a month.

char-grilled *radicchio parcels* with buffalo-milk mozzarella and semi-dried tomatoes

preparation time 15 minutes
cooking time 15 minutes

While mozzarella is traditionally made from buffalo milk, you could use a variety made from cow milk.

8 radicchio leaves
3 buffalo-milk mozzarella (210g), sliced into 16 pieces
16 semi-dried tomato pieces (60g)
16 basil leaves

1 Boil, steam or microwave radicchio until wilted slightly; rinse under cold water, pat dry with absorbent paper.
2 Centre 1 piece mozzarella on each leaf; top with 1 piece tomato and 1 basil leaf. Repeat with 1 piece each mozzarella, tomato and basil; roll radicchio to enclose filling.
3 Grill radicchio parcels on heated oiled grill plate (or grill or barbecue) until browned all over and heated through.

per serving 6.5g fat; 397kJ

Clockwise, from centre left: marinated goat-cheese fetta, kumara and celeriac chips, marinated olives, lavash bread triangles, char-grilled radicchio parcels, rocket and prosciutto frittata and pickled sardines.

thai-flavoured *mussels*

preparation time 10 minutes ■ cooking time 10 minutes

A quartet of Thai seasonings – chilli, lime, lemon grass and coriander – is used to add zest to fresh mussels. Green-lipped New Zealand mussels can be substituted, if desired, although they are larger than black mussels so fewer may be needed for this recipe.

28 mussels (approximately 850g)
2 stalks lemon grass
2 cloves garlic, crushed
2 red Thai chillies, seeded, chopped finely
1/4 cup (60ml) lime juice
2 teaspoons fish sauce
1/4 cup (60ml) water
2 teaspoons sugar
1/4 cup loosely packed coarsely chopped fresh coriander leaves

1 Scrub mussels under cold water; remove beards.

2 Cut lemon grass into 5cm-long thin strips. Combine lemon grass, garlic, chilli, juice, sauce, the water and sugar in large saucepan; stir over heat, without boiling, until sugar dissolves. Bring to a boil, add mussels; cook, covered, about 5 minutes or until mussels open (discard any that do not). Serve sprinkled with coriander.

SERVES 4

per serving 1.1g fat; 235kJ

tuna carpaccio with lemon oil and baby capers

preparation time 10 minutes ■ cooking time 5 minutes

Carpaccio, a dish invented by Arrigo Cipriani of Venice's famed Harry's Bar, is named after a Venetian realist painter of the 1500s. It has come to refer to a dish of raw and thinly sliced marinated beef or fish. Here we use Australian tuna, sliced thinly from a piece of tuna steak by the fishmonger.

400g fresh sashimi-quality thinly sliced tuna
1 tablespoon olive oil
1/4 cup (50g) drained baby capers
2 tablespoons finely shredded lemon rind
1/3 cup (80ml) olive oil, extra
12 slices sourdough bread (420g)

1 Using meat mallet, pound tuna between sheets of plastic wrap until paper-thin; arrange on serving plates in tight concentric circles.

2 Heat oil in small frying pan; cook capers, stirring, until crisp. Drain on absorbent paper.

3 Combine rind with half of the extra oil in small jug; drizzle over tuna. Sprinkle capers over tuna.

4 Brush remaining oil over bread slices both sides; toast both sides in grill pan or under hot grill. Serve with tuna.

SERVES 6

per serving 14.1g fat; 1356kJ

Tasmania is justifiably proud of its Atlantic salmon industry, which, having begun in the early 1980s, now approaches a value of approximately $100 million.

But it's not just the monetary value of the industry that makes it a matter of pride. The waters of the southern and western coastal areas of Tasmania are arguably the cleanest in the world, and in these excellent growing conditions salmon are produced without the use of antibiotics, artificial growth stimulants or other biocidal chemicals. Tasmanian salmon is also free from a number of diseases that are prevalent in overseas salmon industries. The resulting product is a superior fish that is highly prized in the local market and attracts a premium price in the fastidious Japanese market.

Since Atlantic salmon is not native to Australia, the fish are "farmed" in large aquaculture sea-cages, positioned in areas well away from industrial activities that might compromise the purity of the water. Much like any other farmed resource, the entire life cycle takes place in captivity, from the fertilising of the eggs of broodstock fish and their incubation in a "hatchery", through to the young salmons' eventual transfer into the seacages, their development to market size and subsequent harvesting. The harvested fish are gutted, packed in ice, sealed in containers and flown to mainland markets or overseas on the same day as harvesting, ensuring a product of maximum freshness.

There is also a growing local industry in processed salmon products, such as pâté, salmon roe, gravlax and perhaps the best known, smoked Tasmanian salmon, which is prepared using no artificial additives or preservatives and then smoked over a mixture of Australian hardwoods, resulting in a mellow flavour and rich golden colour.

Atlantic salmon is one of the most versatile of all fish for cooking and since Tasmanian aquaculture began to make it readily available, it has become one of Australia's favourite seafoods, featuring as often on the menus of restaurants as it does in family meals. It is as happily served in a traditional manner as it is in the Asian "fusion" dishes that characterise much of modern Australian cuisine. Indeed, the popularity of the product and the success of Tasmania's industry have resulted in similar successful aquaculture ventures in Western Australia and, on a smaller scale, in South Australian waters.

Being rich in heart-friendly Omega-3 polyunsaturated fats, Atlantic salmon remains moist during most cooking methods, but perhaps to truly appreciate its delicate flavour you need to try it in the increasingly popular traditional Japanese ways – as sashimi or sushi.

salmon farmer, trevor dix, tassal ltd, hobart ADRIAN LANDER PHOTO COURTESY JAGUAR AWARDS FOR EXCELLENCE

dawn over a tasmanian salmon farm TASSAL LTD

farmed in the cleanest waters

TASMANIAN SALMON

fresh tasmanian salmon TASSAL LTD

fresh and smoked tasmanian salmon, hobart, tasmania TASSAL LTD

thai beef salad

preparation time 20 minutes ■ cooking time 10 minutes (plus standing time)

In recent years, Australia has embraced Thai cuisine with great enthusiasm. This salad, a particular favourite, is often found on menus as yum nua. It uses Thai basil, also known as holy basil or krapow, which is different from European basil. If you cannot find it, simply increase the quantities of mint and coriander to compensate. Palm sugar is also sold under the name of jaggery.

500g beef scotch fillet
2 medium tomatoes (380g), seeded, sliced thinly
2 Lebanese cucumbers (260g), sliced thinly
4 purple shallots (50g), sliced finely
1/4 cup loosely packed fresh Thai basil leaves
1/4 cup loosely packed fresh spearmint leaves
1/4 cup loosely packed fresh coriander leaves

CHILLI DRESSING
1 red Thai chilli, sliced thinly
1 clove garlic, crushed
2 tablespoons palm sugar
1 tablespoon fish sauce
1 tablespoon soy sauce
1/4 cup (60ml) lime juice

1 Sear beef on heated oiled grill plate (or grill or barbecue) over high heat until browned both sides; beef should be rare. Stand beef, covered, 10 minutes; slice thinly.

2 Just before serving, place beef in large bowl with tomato, cucumber, shallot, basil, mint and coriander; add chilli dressing, toss to combine.

chilli dressing Combine ingredients in small bowl.

SERVES 4

per serving 7.7g fat; 1001kJ

smoked salmon on chilli corn fritters

preparation time 20 minutes ■ cooking time 20 minutes

Tasmania's Atlantic salmon and ocean trout farms have given rise to a delicious array of home-grown smoked fish products, readily available in most supermarkets and fishmongers.

300g sour cream
1 small red onion (100g), chopped finely
1/4 cup finely chopped fresh chives
1/4 cup finely chopped fresh dill
1 cob of corn (400g)
1 egg, beaten lightly
1/3 cup (50g) self-raising flour
1 1/2 tablespoons milk
1 red Thai chilli, seeded, chopped finely
1 tablespoon finely chopped fresh coriander leaves
vegetable oil, for shallow-frying
200g smoked salmon slices

1 Combine sour cream, onion, chives and dill in small bowl.

2 Remove and discard husk and silk from corn; cut kernels from cob. Boil, steam or microwave kernels until just tender, drain on absorbent paper.

3 Combine egg and flour in small bowl; gradually stir in milk. Add corn, chilli and coriander; stir to combine.

4 Heat oil in medium frying pan; cook heaped tablespoons of corn mixture, one at a time, until browned both sides and cooked through. Drain fritters on absorbent paper (you will have eight fritters).

5 Place two fritters on each serving plate; top each serving with equal amounts of sour cream mixture, then salmon slices.

SERVES 4

per serving 46.7g fat; 2409kJ

tips Frozen corn can be substituted for the fresh variety. Don't seed the chillies if you want more heat in the fritters.

duck ravioli in green onion broth

preparation time 30 minutes (plus standing time) ■ cooking time 2 hours

Traditional Italian ravioli can be time-consuming to make. Here we make life simpler by using wonton wrappers and barbecued duck, which can be purchased from Asian barbecue takeaway shops.

1 barbecued duck (1kg)
3 litres (12 cups) water
1 medium brown onion (150g), chopped coarsely
1 trimmed celery stick (75g), chopped coarsely
1 medium carrot (120g), chopped coarsely
4 black peppercorns
25g fresh ginger, chopped coarsely
5 dried shiitake mushrooms
1/4 cup (60ml) boiling water
2 green onions
40 wonton wrappers
1 egg, beaten lightly
2 teaspoons soy sauce

1. Remove meat and skin from duck; reserve meat and bones, discard skin. Chop meat finely, cover; refrigerate until required.
2. Combine bones with the water, brown onion, celery, carrot, peppercorns and ginger in large saucepan; bring to a boil. Simmer, uncovered, 1½ hours; strain through muslin-lined strainer into large bowl. Return stock to same cleaned pan; discard bones and vegetables.
3. Meanwhile, combine mushrooms and the boiling water in small heatproof bowl; stand 20 minutes or until mushrooms are tender, drain. Discard mushroom stems; chop caps finely, reserve.
4. Chop 1 of the green onions finely; combine in medium bowl with meat and mushroom. Place 1 tablespoon of filling in centre of 1 wrapper; brush edges with egg. Top with another wrapper, press edges together to seal. Repeat with remaining wrappers, filling and egg; you will have 20 filled ravioli.
5. Add sauce to stock, bring to a boil; add ravioli, simmer, uncovered, about 10 minutes or until ravioli are just tender.
6. Serve ravioli sprinkled with thinly sliced remaining green onion.

SERVES 10

per serving 6.4g fat; 833kJ

tip Use fresh lasagne sheets or spring roll wrappers in place of wonton wrappers.

grilled *duck liver salad*
with toffeed ginger and wasabi soy dressing

preparation time 20 minutes (plus standing time) ■ cooking time 5 minutes

Mizuna is a slightly mustard-tasting leafy Japanese green. It is teamed here with a wasabi-flavoured dressing. Wasabi is a pungent root vegetable also known as Japanese horseradish, even though it's a member of the mustard family.

4 duck livers (250g)
2 cups (500ml) milk
80g fresh ginger, sliced thinly
1/2 cup (80g) icing sugar mixture
vegetable oil, for deep-frying
1/4 cup (60ml) peanut oil
50g curly endive
40g mizuna
2 tablespoons light soy sauce
1 teaspoon sesame oil
1 teaspoon wasabi

1. Trim and wash livers. Place in medium bowl with milk, cover; refrigerate overnight.
2. Drain livers, rinse under cold water, dry on absorbent paper; cut each liver into three pieces.
3. Coat ginger in icing sugar. Heat vegetable oil in wok or medium saucepan; deep-fry ginger, in batches, until crisp. Drain on absorbent paper.
4. Heat half of the peanut oil in large non-stick frying pan over high heat; sear liver quickly, in batches, both sides, until pieces are well browned but quite rare. Cover to keep warm.
5. Place endive and mizuna in large bowl with combined remaining peanut oil, sauce, sesame oil and wasabi; toss to combine. Divide salad among serving plates; top with liver and ginger.

SERVES 4

per serving 31.2g fat; 1915kJ

tip Chicken livers can be substituted for the duck in this recipe.

beach barbie SCOTT CAMERON

wide ranging – bbq to five-star

AUSTRALIAN BEEF

"Where in the world," wrote Australian novelist Lenny Lower, "will you find anything more sustaining, more inspiring, more satisfying, more invigorating, more absolutely culminating and fulfilling than steak and eggs?" Australian beef has undergone a number of metamorphoses since these lines were written in 1930.

Leaving behind the big country breakfast fry-up, beef moved into haute cuisine – steak diane and the memorable if ill-advised surf 'n' turf – then out again, when large pieces of red meat became unfashionable in the fat-conscious late '80s. Thankfully, lean beef is back on the menu as an invaluable source of protein and iron, but those who truly appreciate their steak know that good beef cannot be completely devoid of fat or it will be tough. The very best tasting Australian beef – the sort that commands premium export prices – has a fine marbling of fat across the grain, not simply a rind of fat around the outer edge.

Beef farming methods and breeds vary quite markedly in Australia. From the massive outback pastoral stations where mustering is done by plane, to the highly intensive feedlot operations producing grain-fed meat specifically for restaurants and the top end of the export market, each region specialises in its own particular product. In the hot, tropical conditions of the north, you are more likely to see Asian breeds of cattle, such as Brahman. In rich cattle country where the rainfall is higher, traditional breeds such as Poll Hereford and Angus are more usual. Smaller, more intensive operations breed specialised cattle, such as Wagyu, which is highly favoured by the Japanese market.

stockman mustering in the northern territory IPL IMAGE GROUP

beef cattle, rockhampton, queensland RAY O'DELL

Long before the famous "shrimp on the barbie" came the arguably more famous "steak on the barbie". There is very little more quintessentially Aussie than a barbecue, whether it's cooked on the latest piece of gas-fired gadgetry or on an old grill propped on a couple of rocks. And a bit of rump or T-bone and the odd banger are as much a part of that tradition as the fire itself.

tina scales, rounding up cattle, queensland MARK COOMBE

potato and leek charlottes with *crab* and atlantic salmon roe

preparation time 1 hour ■ cooking time 40 minutes

2 medium cooked crabs (350g each)
1 large leek (500g)
400g baby spinach leaves
2 medium potatoes (400g)
20g butter
1 small brown onion (80g), chopped finely
1 clove garlic, crushed
2 tablespoons sour cream
50g red salmon roe
16 fresh chervil leaves

MUSTARD BUTTER SAUCE
20g butter
1 small brown onion (80g), chopped finely
1/4 cup (60ml) dry white wine
2 teaspoons Dijon mustard
1/4 cup (60ml) cream
40g butter, extra

1 Grease four 1/2-cup (125ml) metal moulds.

2 Hold crab firmly; slide sharp strong knife under top of shell at back, lever off shell. Remove and discard whitish gills. Rinse the crab under cold water. Cut crab body into quarters; remove meat from shell with fingers. Use a meat mallet or nutcracker to break claws; remove meat. Shred meat, cover; refrigerate until required.

3 Halve leek lengthways; cut each half into thirds. Boil, steam or microwave leek until just tender; rinse under cold water, drain on absorbent paper, separate layers of each leek piece.

4 Boil, steam or microwave spinach until just wilted; squeeze out excess water. Chop spinach coarsely; drain on absorbent paper. Cut potatoes lengthways into thin slices; cut slices in half.

5 Melt butter in small saucepan; cook onion and garlic, stirring, until onion softens, combine with spinach and sour cream in small bowl.

6 Trim potato slices so that each fits, upright, against side of prepared mould. Line moulds, bases and sides, with two alternate layers each of potato and leek (leek should extend 1cm above edge of mould). Spoon equal amounts of spinach mixture inside potato/leek-lined moulds; fold leek over to enclose spinach filling. Bake charlottes, covered, in moderate oven about 25 minutes or until potato is tender. Meanwhile, make mustard butter sauce.

7 Turn charlottes onto serving plates; drizzle with mustard butter sauce, top with crab, sprinkle with roe. Serve charlottes surrounded by a few fresh chervil leaves.

mustard butter sauce Melt butter in small saucepan; cook onion, stirring, until soft. Add wine and mustard, bring to a boil; simmer, uncovered, about 5 minutes or until liquid is reduced by a third. Stir in cream, bring to a boil; simmer, uncovered, about 5 minutes. Whisk in extra butter; cook, stirring, over low heat about 5 minutes or until combined. Strain into small heatproof jug.

SERVES 4

per serving 28.8g fat; 1667kJ

Balmain bugs are a species of sand lobster that proliferate in Australian waters. Substitute lobster or crayfish meat if Balmain bugs are unavailable. Saffron threads contribute a bright yellow colour and distinctive flavour to the dressing. Usually imported from Europe or the Middle East, saffron is now produced in Tasmania, although still in very small quantities.

a cheeky little drop

AUSTRALIAN WINE

If there's one national industry that Australia has really embraced with enthusiasm, it's wine. You can go ballooning or horseriding in wine country, attend a jazz festival, hear the world's great opera singers, dine on fine local produce; you can pick grapes, trample grapes, stay in a vineyard, own a bit of vineyard – and of course, but of course, you can also sample the wine!

Almost as old as the colony itself, Australia's wine industry has expanded into a billion-dollar business and, after 175 years of continuous grape-growing and winemaking, wine is now made in every state of Australia.

How did this come about, when only 30 years ago, the only wine in the average Australian household was a sweet sherry kept somewhere deep in the recesses of the sideboard? The answers to this question are many and varied, but a seminal moment must surely have been the launch, in the early 1970s, of the wine cask, Australia's gift to the world. Backed by imaginative marketing, the budget-priced "bag in the box" introduced a whole generation to the delights of wine with meals. Casks were happily carried to parties, picnics, barbecues, beaches and even to the proliferating BYO restaurants. It might now seem rather unsophisticated (although interestingly, about 50 per cent of the wine consumed in Australia still comes from a cask), but it certainly raised the general level of wine awareness in consumers so that, having caught our attention, the winemakers could set about educating our palates.

And set about it they did. The national penchant for a sweet white Moselle gave way to a much broader range of taste and, although the extraordinary love affair with Chardonnay continues, consumption of both Shiraz and Cabernet Sauvignon is growing and there is a steadily increasing interest in lesser known varietals, as well as in a range of excellent quality sparkling white wines that no longer need to apologise for not being "Champagne".

barossa grapes, south australia ADAM BRUZZONE

vineyards, hunter valley, new south wales OLIVER STREWE ATC

wine tasting, clare valley, south australia MILTON WORDLEY

Enthusiasm for Australian wine is not limited to local consumers, however. Wine exports increase significantly every year and Australian wines are being sought by a growing number of new markets, including several European countries. Are the descendants of those very first imported grapevines that started life with the fledgling colony now producing wine that will travel full circle? Here's cheers to that idea!

wirra wirra winery, south australia MILTON WORDLEY

lobster with flavoured butter and *lemon grass* mash

preparation time 20 minutes (plus refrigeration and freezing time)
cooking time 30 minutes

LIFESAVERS, BONDI BEACH, SYDNEY
Peter Solness

2 medium live lobsters (approximately 1.5kg)
100g butter, softened
2 tablespoons coarsely chopped fresh Vietnamese mint leaves
2 tablespoons coarsely chopped fresh Thai basil leaves
1 tablespoon coarsely chopped garlic chives
1 clove garlic, crushed
2 stalks lemon grass
4 large potatoes (1.2kg), chopped coarsely
50g fresh ginger, sliced thickly
2½ cups (625ml) milk

1. Place lobsters in freezer for 2 hours; this is the most humane way of killing them. Place lobster, upside down, on chopping board; cut through chest and tail. Turn lobster around and cut through head; pull lobster halves apart. Discard white gills, the light-green liver and grey thread running down centre back of tail. Refrigerate, covered, until required.
2. Combine butter, mint, basil, chives and garlic in small bowl, cover; refrigerate.
3. Cut each lemon grass stalk into three pieces. Combine lemon grass, potato, ginger and milk in medium saucepan. Bring to a boil; simmer, covered, stirring occasionally, about 25 minutes or until potato is tender. Strain potato mixture over medium bowl; reserve ¼ cup spiced milk. Discard ginger and lemon grass; return potato to pan. Mash over low heat until smooth; stir in reserved spiced milk.
4. Meanwhile, grill lobster on heated oiled grill plate (or grill or barbecue) until browned and just changed in colour.
5. Serve lobster, topped with flavoured butter, on lemon grass mash.

SERVES 4

per serve 30g fat; 3177kJ

tip Reheat mash in the microwave oven, if necessary, to make it fluffy and soft.

In this recipe, one of Australia's favourite forms of seafood is given an Oriental flavour-boost with the inclusion of Asian herbs in both the delicious butter sauce and the bed of mashed potato.

salt-crusted *barramundi* on baby bok choy with *red curry* sauce

preparation time 25 minutes ■ cooking time 40 minutes

4 whole baby barramundi (1.2kg)
3 cloves garlic, sliced thinly
1 tablespoon garlic salt
2 tablespoons sea salt
2 tablespoons peanut oil
4 green onions
50g fresh ginger
1/4 cup finely shredded fresh coriander leaves
1/4 cup (70g) red curry paste
3/4 cup (180ml) vegetable stock
1/2 cup (125ml) water
1 cup (250ml) coconut milk
2 kaffir lime leaves, torn
500g baby bok choy, trimmed, halved

1. Preheat oven to hot.
2. Score fish three times both sides; place on oiled wire rack over large baking dish. Press garlic into cuts, sprinkle with combined salts, drizzle with half of the oil. Roast fish in hot oven, uncovered, about 30 minutes or until skin is crisp and fish is cooked as desired.
3. Meanwhile, slice onions and ginger into 5cm-long thin strips. Toss in small bowl with coriander; reserve.
4. Heat remaining oil in wok or large frying pan; stir-fry paste about 2 minutes or until fragrant. Add stock, the water, coconut milk and lime leaves, bring to a boil; simmer, uncovered, 5 minutes. Add bok choy; stir-fry until just wilted.
5. Serve fish with bok choy and red curry sauce; sprinkle with reserved coriander mixture.

SERVES 4

per serving 29g fat; 1770kJ

Highly prized for its white, tender flesh, barramundi is native to the warm waters of northern Australia where it's farmed as well as harvested from the wild. If necessary, you can substitute any firm-fleshed, non-oily fish.

Not so long ago, there was a famous and funny advertisement for lamb. Forced to choose between a date with heart-throb Tom Cruise or a lamb roast with the family, an attractive young woman chooses the lamb roast. It made us all laugh, but perhaps with more than a little recognition that a great many of us would have made the same choice. A big leg of roast lamb with three vegies, gravy and mint sauce – it's the meal that many remember fondly from childhood, the meal that mothers still cook when the family comes home to celebrate, *the* traditional Australian meal.

Of course, there's a great deal more to the lamb industry than lamb roast, and today's more eclectic tastes mean that another generation might just as well become nostalgic over a lamb stir-fry. But one thing is certain, Australians love their lamb – the domestic market consumes 76 per cent of all the lamb produced in Australia, an enormous amount, considering that the export figure is some 55,000 tonnes a year.

Sheep first came to Australia with the First Fleet in 1788, 29 of them in all, a number that has grown today to about 120 million! The first commercial successes were eventually made with Merino wool and for many years the wool industry, for which Australia became justifiably famous, rather eclipsed the meat industry. While Merinos are, in fact, suitable for meat, the large lean lambs preferred by the market today, both domestically and abroad, are usually a crossbreed of Merino and a meat-producing variety.

While the sheep industry can be said to range across every state and territory of the country, from the arid and semi-arid pastoral leases of South Australia and outback Queensland to the higher rainfall areas of New South Wales, Victoria and Tasmania, prime lamb production is actually more specifically confined to good pastoral conditions and areas with reliable rainfall.

However, lamb production is really only a part of the story and in fact, mutton (a little older than lamb and considered by many to be much more flavourful) is actually the second largest meat export, following beef.

Although the distance of Australia from export markets is something of a disadvantage, this also has its positive side. As with so much of our primary industry, Australia's very isolation and strict quarantine laws mean that the lamb industry is free of many of the diseases that plague other markets.

So whether it's a succulent loin chop, a lean fillet or the traditional roast, if it's Australian lamb, you can be sure it's the best in the world – and certainly worth at least *postponing* a date with Tom Cruise.

r. and i.j. bergan, top quality butchers, wahroonga, new south wales SCOTT CAMERON

sheep farmer and his working dog AUSTRALIAN TOURIST COMMISSION

an australian favourite

PRIME LAMB

aditional lamb roast

sheep grazing, south australia AUSTRALIAN TOURIST COMMISSION

char-grilled *seafood salad* with gremolata dressing

preparation time 30 minutes (plus marinating time)
cooking time 20 minutes

HINCHINBROOK ISLAND, TROPICAL NORTH QUEENSLAND
Tourism Queensland

24 large uncooked prawns (1kg)
500g squid hoods
500g cleaned baby octopus
1/3 cup (80ml) olive oil
2 tablespoons finely chopped lemon rind
2 cloves garlic, chopped finely
1 medium green cucumber (170g)
100g mixed cress leaves
2 tablespoons lemon juice
2 tablespoons coarsely chopped fresh flat-leaf parsley

1. Shell and devein prawns, leaving heads and tails intact. Cut squid in half lengthways; score inside surface of each piece, cut into 5cm-wide strips. Remove and discard heads from octopus.
2. Combine seafood in large bowl with 1 tablespoon of the oil, 1 teaspoon of the rind and half the garlic, cover; refrigerate 3 hours or overnight.
3. Cook seafood, in batches, on heated oiled grill plate (or grill or barbecue) until prawns are just changed in colour, and squid and octopus are tender and browned all over.
4. Using vegetable peeler, slice cucumber into ribbons. Combine cucumber with cress in medium bowl.
5. Combine juice and parsley with remaining oil, rind and garlic in screw-top jar; shake well.
6. Serve seafood on cucumber-cress mixture; drizzle with dressing.

SERVES 6

per serving 14.7g fat; 1238kJ

Gremolata is an aromatic combination of lemon rind, garlic and parsley, traditionally used as a garnish for the Italian braised veal dish, osso bucco. Here, its gutsy flavour adds zest to a seafood salad.

seared *tuna* niçoise *salad* with anchovy dressing

preparation time 25 minutes ■ cooking time 25 minutes

12 quail eggs
200g baby green beans, trimmed
10 new potatoes (400g), sliced thinly
olive oil, for shallow-frying
500g piece sashimi tuna
1 small red onion (80g), sliced thinly
250g cherry tomatoes
1/3 cup (60g) niçoise olives
1/4 cup (40g) caperberries
2 tablespoons finely shredded fresh basil leaves

ANCHOVY DRESSING

1 egg
1 clove garlic, quartered
2 tablespoons lemon juice
1 teaspoon Dijon mustard
6 drained anchovy fillets
1/2 cup (125ml) light olive oil
2 tablespoons milk

1 Place eggs in small saucepan of cold water; bring to a boil then remove from heat immediately. Drain; rinse eggs under cold water. Drain, peel and halve eggs.

2 Boil, steam or microwave beans and potato, separately, until just tender. Rinse, separately, under cold water; drain.

3 Heat oil in medium frying pan; shallow-fry potato, in batches, until browned, drain on absorbent paper.

4 Cut tuna into 2cm-thick steaks; cut each steak into quarters. Cook tuna on heated oiled grill plate (or grill or barbecue) about 30 seconds each side or until just seared on the outside.

5 Arrange tuna, beans, onion, tomatoes and potato on serving platter; scatter with egg halves, olives and caperberries, drizzle with anchovy dressing, sprinkle with basil.

anchovy dressing Blend or process egg, garlic, juice, mustard and anchovies until smooth. While motor is operating, gradually add oil; process until mixture is thickened. Just before drizzling over salad, stir in milk.

SERVES 4

per serving 62.1g fat; 3448kJ

tip Tuna should just be cooked long enough to sear the outside; it will still be uncooked in the centre. Tuna is best served this way because, if cooked completely through, it becomes dry and unpalatable.

Australian sashimi tuna is of the highest quality and much sought-after by the Japanese market. Here it is served lightly seared instead of raw, and added to the classic Mediterranean salad that takes its name from Nice on the French Riviera.

aussie *fish 'n' chips*

preparation time 30 minutes (plus refrigeration time) ■ cooking time 30 minutes

DOYLES RESTAURANT AT WATSONS BAY, SYDNEY, NEW SOUTH WALES
Hamilton Lund ATC

1½ cups (225g) self-raising flour
1 egg
1½ cups (375ml) beer
5 large potatoes (1.5kg)
vegetable oil, for deep-frying
12 flathead fillets (660g)

TARTARE SAUCE
200ml crème fraîche
2 teaspoons finely grated lemon rind
2 teaspoons lemon juice
2 tablespoons finely chopped sweet gherkins
2 tablespoons drained capers, chopped finely
1 tablespoon finely chopped fresh chives
1 red Thai chilli, seeded, chopped finely

1. Whisk flour, egg and beer together in medium bowl until smooth, cover; refrigerate 1 hour.
2. Meanwhile, preheat oven to moderate. Cut peeled potatoes into 1cm slices; cut slices into 1cm-thick chips. Pat potato chips completely dry with absorbent paper.
3. Heat oil in large saucepan; deep-fry chips, in batches, until browned and cooked through. Place chips on absorbent paper on large oven tray; place, uncovered, in moderate oven.
4. Reheat oil. Dip fish in beer batter, drain away excess batter. Deep-fry fish, in batches, until browned and crisp.
5. Divide fish and chips among serving plates; serve with tartare sauce.

tartare sauce Combine ingredients in medium bowl; mix well.

SERVES 4

per serving 103.4g fat; 6484kJ

tip Double-fry chips to allow the potato to cook through without over-browning. The best varieties of potato to use for chips are bintje, nicola, patrone or russet burbank.

A light beer batter is used to coat the fish in this universal favourite. The accompanying tartare sauce uses a base of crème fraîche, a cultured cream product that can be made at home by combining sour cream or buttermilk with pure cream and allowing it to ferment.

ildman river, kakadu national park, northern territory IPL IMAGE GROUP

barramundi dreaming

AUSTRALIA'S NATIVE FISH

Barramundi is an Aboriginal word meaning "river fish with large scales". Long before white settlement began in Australia, these native fish were caught in the traditional manner – speared in the warm, shallow waters of a tidal creek or estuary, having been attracted to the light of a burning torch. Wrapped in wild ginger leaves or sheets of paperbark and baked quickly in the ashes of a hot fire, how could fresh fish taste any better?

Barramundi is a popular table and angling fish, not least because it is associated with the remote and beautiful landscapes of the tropical north of Australia, from the Kimberley in Western Australia, to Kakadu in the Northern Territory and the pristine wilderness of Far North Queensland. As it is a native fish, for non-indigenous anglers there is a quota on the number and size of the barramundi that can be taken.

In reality, most of the barramundi that we see in the markets is probably farmed. Darwin, Weipa, Cairns, Innisfail, Townsville, Bundaberg and Adelaide have all established successful barramundi farms, specialising in "plate-sized" (about 400g) whole baby barramundi that are available all year round. Wild-caught barramundi are generally only available for a limited season and are usually larger than the farmed variety, averaging up to 4 kilograms, although the Australian record stands at a little over 22 kilograms! For this reason wild fish are usually filleted. Farmed baby barramundi are always sold whole.

Commercial farming of barramundi began in Australia in the mid 1980s and production has increased rapidly over the past decade so that the value of the farmed product now equals the value of the wild catch, and is worth millions of dollars. Barramundi is an ideal fish to farm because it can live in fresh or salt water and grows quickly. Its tough scaly exterior means that it is also very robust.

Several different farming methods are used in Australia. Depending on the region, fish are either farmed in brackish ponds, held in sea-cages in estuarine

rramundi cooked in paperbark

the big barramundi, queensland TOURISM QUEENSLAND

waters or produced indoors in an artificially controlled environment which allows for year round production.

But if all this talk of farming just seems too unromantic, there's always a billabong somewhere in the Top End at the end of the wet season, where it's going on dusk and the wild barramundi of your dreams is the one that got away.

lime and chilli *laksa*

preparation time 30 minutes ■ cooking time 40 minutes

You will need a bunch of fresh coriander weighing 100g, including roots and stems, for this recipe.

2 tablespoons peanut oil
3¼ cups (800ml) coconut milk
1 litre (4 cups) chicken stock
¼ cup (60ml) lime juice
1 tablespoon palm sugar
10 kaffir lime leaves, torn
600g fried tofu, chopped
500g baby bok choy, trimmed, quartered
375g rice stick noodles
2 cups (160g) bean sprouts
1 Lebanese cucumber (130g), seeded, sliced thinly
2 green onions, sliced thinly
2 tablespoons fresh coriander leaves
2 tablespoons fresh Vietnamese mint leaves

LAKSA PASTE

1 tablespoon shrimp paste
¼ cup (36g) grated fresh galangal
3 large red Thai chillies, chopped coarsely
1 tablespoon ground coriander
2 teaspoons ground cumin
1 teaspoon ground turmeric
1 medium brown onion (150g), chopped coarsely
3 cloves garlic, quartered
⅓ cup coarsely chopped coriander roots and stems
¼ cup coarsely chopped fresh lemon grass

1. Make laksa paste first. Heat oil in large saucepan; cook paste, stirring, until fragrant. Add coconut milk, stock, juice, sugar and lime leaves; bring to a boil. Simmer, uncovered, 25 minutes; stir tofu and bok choy into laksa mixture.
2. Meanwhile, place noodles in large heatproof bowl, cover with boiling water, stand until just tender; drain. Divide noodles among serving bowls; top with laksa mixture, sprinkle with sprouts, cucumber, onion, coriander and mint.

laksa paste Blend or process ingredients until mixture forms a smooth paste.

SERVES 4

per serving 74.5g fat; 4701kJ

tip Serve accompanied with sambal oelek and wedges of lime.

Laksa, with its distinctive combination of coconut milk, lemon grass and chilli, comes originally from Malaysia and Singapore. However, so ubiquitous is this spicy soup on restaurant menus and in noodle bars all over the country that Australians have almost adopted it as their own.

lamb kofta

with hummus and tabbouleh

preparation time 1 hour (plus standing time) ■ cooking time 20 minutes

LEBANESE PASTRIES FROM SWEET LAND, HARRIS PARK, SYDNEY
Isabella Lettini

1/2 cup (80g) burghul
1kg minced lamb
1 small brown onion (80g), chopped finely
1 teaspoon allspice
1 clove garlic, crushed
1 cup (75g) stale breadcrumbs
1 egg, beaten lightly
200g plain yogurt
1/4 cup finely chopped fresh mint leaves

HUMMUS
2 x 300g cans chickpeas, drained
1 teaspoon salt
1 clove garlic, quartered
1/3 cup (80ml) tahini
1/4 cup (60ml) lemon juice
1/3 cup (80ml) water

TABBOULEH
1/4 cup (40g) burghul
2 medium tomatoes (380g), seeded, chopped finely
4 cups coarsely chopped fresh flat-leaf parsley
1 small red onion (100g), chopped finely
2 tablespoons lemon juice
2 tablespoons olive oil

1. Cover burghul with cold water in small bowl; stand 20 minutes or until burghul softens. Drain burghul, squeezing with hands to remove as much water as possible.
2. Using hands, combine burghul with lamb, onion, allspice, garlic, breadcrumbs and egg in large bowl. Divide mixture into 12 balls; mould balls around skewers to form sausage shape. Cook on heated oiled grill plate (or grill or barbecue) until browned all over and cooked through.
3. Serve kofta with hummus, tabbouleh and combined yogurt and mint.

hummus Blend or process ingredients until almost smooth.

tabbouleh Cover burghul with cold water in small bowl; stand 10 minutes or until burghul softens. Drain burghul, squeezing with hands to remove as much water as possible. Combine burghul in large bowl with remaining ingredients.

SERVES 6

per serving 33.2g fat; 2575kJ

tips Soak the skewers in cold water for at least an hour to prevent them from splintering and scorching.
Lamb can be replaced with minced beef or chicken, if you prefer.

Variants of the word "kofta", which covers a range of minced or ground meat dishes, can be found in countries as diverse as Greece, Turkey, India, Syria and Lebanon. Lamb is the traditional Middle-Eastern choice and in Australia, where lamb is so readily available and popular, the perfect choice as well.

ud crabs in blackbean sauce

feast from the mangroves

MUD CRABS

True mud crab enthusiasts will set you straight: why fiddle about with the spindly limbs of other crustaceans when you can have such an easy meal from the giant claws of the mud crab? Those enormous claws certainly seem to be the distinguishing feature of *Scylla serrata*, also known as the mangrove crab.

Aboriginal legend has it that in the Dreamtime the mud crab had pathetic little nippers which he exchanged for powerful claws, glued in place with wattle gum. Impatient to try them out, the foolish creature wouldn't wait until the gum was dry and to this day, the mud crab has a tendency to lose his claws, especially when threatened, although they will grow back eventually.

Although associated largely with Queensland and the Northern Territory, mud crabs are found in tropical to warm temperate waters around Australia's northern coastline from Exmouth in Western Australia to the mouth of the Bega River in southern New South Wales. They are sold live in fish markets around Australia and are also exported.

As their name implies, they inhabit mudflats and mangrove forests, sheltered muddy estuaries and the tidal reaches of some rivers, feeding on molluscs and other crustaceans of various types. What many people do not realise is that in order to grow, mudcrabs must regularly shed their shells, in the same way as a snake. After walking out of the old shell, they are protected by only a soft clear membrane, which is stretched by the ingestion of water and hardens into a new, larger shell. This process explains why you can sometimes purchase what appears to be an "empty" crab – the crab

mangroves at hope vale aboriginal community, north queensland TOURISM QUEENSLAND

catch-a-crab tours, cairns TOURISM QUEENSLAND

inside has not yet grown into its new shell. A good fishmonger will be able to tell you if a crab is full or "empty".

Mud crabs are caught in simple wire traps baited with fish heads or meat. Because the areas the crabs inhabit can be so picturesque, several tourist companies run popular crab-catching tours – a quiet boat trip through tranquil backwaters and primeval mangrove forests teeming with birdlife ... and the freshest lunch imaginable!

unpacking mud crabs, sydney fish markets SCOTT CAMERON

tandoori chicken

with paprika oil and minted yogurt

preparation time 30 minutes (plus marinating time)
cooking time 30 minutes

You will need about 1kg of unshelled peas for this recipe.

ASIAN BARBECUED MEAT SHOP, SYDNEY
Graham Monro ATC

700g chicken breast fillets, sliced
1 teaspoon ground turmeric
1 teaspoon ground cumin
2 cloves garlic, crushed
1 teaspoon garam masala
1 tablespoon sweet paprika
1/2 cup (125ml) peanut oil
1/3 cup firmly packed fresh mint leaves
200ml plain yogurt
1 medium cauliflower (1.5kg), trimmed
cooking-oil spray
2 1/4 cups (350g) shelled fresh peas
2 small red onions (200g), cut into wedges

1 Combine chicken, turmeric, cumin, garlic, garam masala, 3 teaspoons of the paprika, and 1 tablespoon of the oil in large bowl, cover; refrigerate 3 hours or overnight.

2 Blend or process mint and yogurt until smooth.

3 Preheat oven to hot. Cut cauliflower into florets; place in single layer, on greased oven tray, spray lightly with cooking-oil spray. Cook, uncovered, in hot oven about 30 minutes or until browned and just tender.

4 Meanwhile, boil, steam or microwave peas until tender; drain. Heat remaining oil and paprika, stirring, in small saucepan; cool, strain.

5 Heat 1 tablespoon of the paprika oil in wok or large frying pan; stir-fry chicken and onion, in batches, until chicken is cooked through. Return chicken mixture to same wok with peas; stir-fry until hot.

6 Serve chicken and peas with cauliflower; drizzle with remaining hot paprika oil and minted yogurt.

SERVES 4

per serving 36.6g fat; 2502kJ
tips Serve with plain steamed basmati rice or homemade naan. Cauliflower can also be shallow-fried or deep-fried.

The term "tandoori" comes from the Hindi word tandoor, a clay oven used in northern India to cook meats and breads. The term has migrated around the world and its meaning has broadened to describe meat marinated in a mixture of Indian spices that usually includes either paprika or natural food dye, giving a reddish colour to the finished dish.

char-grilled *baby vegetable* salad and *pesto* with *polenta triangles*

preparation time 30 minutes (plus marinating time) ■ cooking time 1 hour (plus standing time)

4 baby eggplants (240g)
2 baby fennel (250g)
250g cherry tomatoes
18 baby zucchini (185g)
½ cup (125ml) lemon juice
½ cup (125ml) olive oil
4 cloves garlic, crushed
500g bunch baby beetroot, trimmed
2 cobs of corn (800g)
400g baby carrots, trimmed
350g tiny new potatoes, halved

POLENTA TRIANGLES

½ cup (125ml) vegetable stock
2 cups (500ml) water
1 cup (250ml) milk
1½ cups (255g) polenta
20g butter
¾ cup (60g) finely grated parmesan cheese
50g seeded black olives, chopped finely

PESTO

1¾ cups firmly packed fresh basil leaves
1 clove garlic, quartered
¼ cup (40g) pine nuts, toasted
½ cup (40g) coarsely grated parmesan cheese
¾ cup (180ml) olive oil

1 Slice each eggplant lengthways into three pieces; halve each fennel lengthways.

2 Combine eggplant, fennel, tomatoes and zucchini in large bowl with juice, oil and garlic; cover, refrigerate 3 hours or overnight.

3 Preheat oven to moderately hot. Place beetroot in large oiled baking dish; roast, covered, in moderately hot oven 15 minutes.

4 Meanwhile, remove husk and silk from corn; cut cobs into 3cm pieces.

5 Add corn, carrot and potato to baking dish with beetroot; roast, covered, in moderately hot oven 30 minutes, turning halfway during cooking.

6 Peel beetroot; reserve. Cook corn, carrot, potato and drained marinated vegetables, in batches, on heated oiled grill plate (or grill or barbecue) until browned and just tender.

7 Serve vegetables with polenta triangles and pesto.

polenta triangles Heat stock, the water and milk in large saucepan (do not boil). Add polenta; cook, stirring, about 2 minutes or until liquid is absorbed and mixture thickens. Stir in butter, cheese and olives. Spoon polenta into 23cm-square slab cake pan, pressing firmly to ensure even thickness. When cool, cover; refrigerate about 3 hours or until firm. Turn polenta onto board, trim edges; cut into quarters, cut each quarter into four triangles. Grill polenta on heated oiled grill plate (or grill or barbecue) until browned all over.

pesto Blend or process basil, garlic, pine nuts and cheese until almost smooth; with motor operating, gradually add oil until pesto is thickened and smooth.

SERVES 4

per serving 51.3g fat; 4036kJ (excluding pesto);
pesto, per tablespoon (20g) 14.3g fat; 559kJ

tip Polenta can be made a day ahead and kept, covered, in the refrigerator.

Australians love a barbecue and this recipe, with its Italian influence, adds a welcome vegetarian accent to the national obsession. We used red-skinned, waxy pontiac potatoes, but any salad potato can be substituted.

kangaroo fillet with potato timbale and beetroot

preparation time 50 minutes ■ cooking time 1 hour 30 minutes

CAMPING NEAR PEBBLY BEACH, NEW SOUTH WALES
John Gunter

1kg beetroot, trimmed
1/2 cup (125ml) buttermilk
2 tablespoons finely shredded fresh mint leaves
4 medium potatoes (800g), sliced thinly
1/3 cup (25g) finely grated parmesan cheese
2/3 cup (160ml) cream
1/3 cup (80g) sour cream
1 clove garlic, crushed
4 kangaroo fillets (750g)
2 tablespoons green peppercorns, chopped finely
1/4 cup (60g) seeded mustard

1. Preheat oven to moderately hot.
2. Wrap beetroot in foil, place on oven tray; roast in moderately hot oven about 1 1/2 hours or until tender.
3. Peel beetroot; blend or process until pureed, stir in buttermilk and mint. Cover to keep warm.
4. Meanwhile, oil four 1-cup (250ml) metal moulds. Layer potato and cheese in prepared moulds; divide combined cream, sour cream and garlic among moulds. Bake, uncovered, in moderately hot oven about 1 hour or until potatoes are tender. Stand 5 minutes before turning onto serving plates.
5. Coat kangaroo in combined peppercorns and mustard. Cook kangaroo on heated oiled grill plate (or grill or barbecue) about 2 minutes each side until seared, stand 5 minutes before slicing.
6. Serve kangaroo with beetroot puree and potato timbale.

SERVES 4

per serving 30.5g fat; 2919kJ

tip Kangaroo should remain rare in the centre after cooking; it must be rested before slicing to prevent the meat becoming tough and chewy.

In recent years, kangaroo meat has become readily available as a game meat, and its low-cholesterol leanness has made it popular in modern restaurants. We've teamed it with green peppercorns, now grown in tropical north Queensland and sometimes available fresh, but more easily found canned in brine.

roast pork rack with spinach and walnut *pesto*

preparation time 15 minutes ■ cooking time 1 hour 30 minutes

1 rack of pork (6 cutlets), rind intact (approximately 1.25kg)
2 tablespoons olive oil
1 teaspoon salt
2kg pumpkin

SPINACH AND WALNUT PESTO
300g spinach, trimmed
½ cup (50g) walnut pieces, toasted
1 clove garlic, quartered
2 tablespoons coarsely grated parmesan cheese
1 tablespoon lemon juice
½ cup (125ml) olive oil

1 Preheat oven to very hot.

2 Place pork, rind-side up, on oiled wire rack over large baking dish. Drizzle with half the oil; rub salt evenly over rind. Roast pork, uncovered, in very hot oven about 30 minutes or until rind is well browned. Reduce temperature to moderate; roast pork, covered loosely with foil, about 1 hour or until cooked through.

3 Meanwhile, cut pumpkin into 3cm-thick wedges; place in large baking dish, drizzle with remaining oil. Roast, uncovered, about 50 minutes or until browned and tender.

4 Slice pork into cutlets; serve with pumpkin wedges and spinach and walnut pesto.

spinach and walnut pesto Boil, steam or microwave spinach until just wilted; drain, squeeze out excess liquid with hands. Blend or process spinach, walnuts, garlic, cheese and juice until almost smooth; with motor operating, gradually add oil until pesto is smooth.

SERVES 6

per serving 65.5g fat; 3590kJ
tip We left the skin on the pumpkin, but peel it if you prefer.

Queensland Blue is a local pumpkin variety much admired for its firm texture and depth of flavour, and famous for its use in pumpkin scones. Here, it marries well with the bold flavours in the pork and pesto.

Although southern bluefin tuna have been caught off the coast of South Australia for many years and there has long been a thriving fishing industry centred in Port Lincoln, the actual farming of wild-born tuna is a relatively recent innovation.

The first experimental tuna farm was established at Port Lincoln in 1991 to ascertain if wild southern bluefin tuna would survive capture and continue to thrive and grow in captivity. This eventually proved a success and today, southern bluefin tuna farming, unique to the state of South Australia, has become the single most valuable sector of the state's aquaculture industry.

Unlike the Atlantic salmon industry of Tasmania, tuna farming still involves a combination of both wild and captive fish. Under a very strict quota system to avoid overfishing, tuna for aquaculture are caught from the wild in the waters of the Great Australian Bight, when they are between three and six years old and weigh up to 20 kilograms. Originally, the fish were caught with rods and lines, but to increase the yield and minimise damage, these days they are captured in large nets, transferred to sea-cages and towed very gently to the floating farm sites around Port Lincoln. These "farms" are actually enormous double-netted circular pontoons, some 30-40 metres in diameter, which can hold as many as 2000 fish. The outer net extends almost to the sea floor and is used to keep predators, mainly seals and sharks, from the captive tuna. In these floating pens, the fish are fattened up for the market, being fed a rich daily diet of pilchards, mackerel and pelletised supplements for three to six months, by which time they will have just about doubled their capture weight. One of the great advantages of farming is that the fish can be held until they are in perfect condition and at exactly the desired weight for the market.

The Asian influence on Australian eating habits and, in particular, the growing interest in Japanese sushi and sashimi, mean that Australians are eating an increasing amount of their own fresh tuna, but by far the greater proportion of the farmed bluefin tuna is still airfreighted whole to Japan for the sashimi market, where each fish is individually auctioned. A smaller part of the harvest is frozen in Port Lincoln and then sent by ship to Japan.

Port Lincoln also has a flourishing tuna canning industry and the increasingly sophisticated canned products, enthusiastic marketing and the recognition of tuna as one of the "oily fish", rich in Omega-3 polyunsaturates, mean that tuna, in one form or another, is now well and truly established on the Australian menu.

sushi kim, sydney fish markets, new south wales SCOTT CAMERON

na pens, port lincoln harbour, eyre peninsula, south australia MILTON WORDLEY

hook, line and sashimi

TUNA FISHING

transferring tuna to pens, eyre peninsula, south australia MILTON WORDLEY

char-grilled tuna steak with vegetables and lemor

veal t-bone with buttered spinach and *roast tomatoes*

preparation time 10 minutes ■ cooking time 1 hour 20 minutes

12 small tomatoes on vine (1.5kg)
4 veal T-bone steaks (850g)
50g butter
2 cloves garlic, crushed
900g spinach, trimmed
1/4 cup finely shredded fresh basil leaves
2 tablespoons olive oil
50g pecorino cheese, shaved

1. Preheat oven to moderately slow.
2. Place tomatoes in large oiled baking dish. Roast, uncovered, in moderately slow oven about 1 hour or until tomatoes soften.
3. Meanwhile, grill veal on heated oiled grill plate (or grill or barbecue) until browned both sides and cooked as desired.
4. Melt butter in large saucepan; cook garlic and spinach until spinach is just wilted.
5. Serve veal with spinach and tomatoes; spoon over combined basil and oil, sprinkle with cheese.

SERVES 4

per serving 26g fat; 1804kJ

The green, fertile pastures of Queensland's Darling Downs produce Australia's highest-quality, most sought-after veal. Its delicate flavour is highlighted by the simple fresh taste of vine-ripened tomatoes and spinach.

slow-roasted *lamb shanks* with caramelised red onion and *white bean puree*

preparation time 20 minutes ■ cooking time 4 hours 30 minutes

1 tablespoon olive oil
8 French-trimmed lamb shanks (approximately 1.2kg)
1 tablespoon sugar
1½ cups (375ml) dry red wine
2 cups (500ml) beef stock
3 cloves garlic, crushed
20g butter
1 small brown onion (80g), chopped finely
1 trimmed celery stick (75g), chopped finely
1 tablespoon plain flour
1 tablespoon tomato paste
4 sprigs fresh rosemary, chopped coarsely

WHITE BEAN PUREE

2 x 400g cans cannellini beans, rinsed, drained
1 cup (250ml) chicken stock
4 cloves garlic, quartered
1 tablespoon lemon juice
2 tablespoons olive oil

CARAMELISED ONION

40g butter
2 medium red onions (340g), sliced thinly
¼ cup (50g) brown sugar
¼ cup (60ml) raspberry vinegar

1 Preheat oven to slow.

2 Heat oil in large flameproof baking dish; cook shanks until browned all over. Stir in sugar, wine, stock and garlic; bring to a boil. Transfer lamb to slow oven; roast, covered, about 4 hours, turning twice during cooking.

3 Remove lamb from dish; cover to keep warm. Pour pan liquids into large heatproof jug.

4 Return dish to heat, melt butter; cook onion and celery, stirring, until celery is just tender. Stir in flour; cook, stirring, 2 minutes. Add reserved pan liquids, tomato paste and rosemary; bring to a boil. Simmer, uncovered, stirring until mixture boils and thickens; strain wine sauce into large heatproof jug.

5 Serve lamb with wine sauce, white bean puree and caramelised onion.

white bean puree Combine beans and stock in medium saucepan, bring to a boil; simmer, covered, 20 minutes. Uncover; simmer, stirring occasionally, about 10 minutes or until liquid is absorbed. Blend or process beans, garlic and juice until almost smooth; with motor operating, gradually add oil until mixture forms a smooth puree.

caramelised onion Melt butter in medium saucepan; cook onion, stirring, about 15 minutes or until browned and soft. Stir in sugar and vinegar; cook, stirring, about 15 minutes or until onion is caramelised.

SERVES 4

per serving 50.6g fat; 3635kJ

Sunday lamb roasts have been much loved by Australians for generations. As tastes and habits change, lamb has remained a favourite, embracing a number of new cuts and inventive flavour combinations. The term "French-trimmed" means as much fat, gristle and sinew as possible have been removed. These shanks are sometimes marketed as "lamb drumsticks".

fishing for the future

WESTERN ROCK LOBSTER

The next time you sit down to a plate of fresh seafood, spare a brief thought as to whether your grandchildren or great-grandchildren will be able to do the same.

Using modern technology and improved techniques, we can catch more fish than at any other time in history, but it is also becoming alarmingly apparent that if we continue to harvest the seas in the way that we are doing now, there may not always be any fish to catch – however technological our methods might be.

The answer to depleted fish stocks is to develop sustainable fishing industries and in implementing this solution, the Western Australian Rock Lobster fishery is a world-leader.

The waters off the coast of Western Australia are bountiful. Vast and unpolluted, the fishing grounds and aquaculture farms of the state provide a tempting array of seafood, from finfish and prawns to shellfish and western rock lobsters. Internationally recognised as the world's premium cold water lobster, western rock lobster is exported live or frozen to Asia, the United States and Europe. It is the most significant single species fishery in Australia, generating exports of around $300 million a year. More importantly for the future of such a lucrative industry, the Western Australian Western Rock Lobster fishery is also the first fishery in the world to receive Marine Stewardship Council (MSC) accreditation as a sustainable, well managed fishery, and the right to market its lobster under the MSC promoted Eco-label.

The MSC is a non-profit international certification organisation dedicated to the long term sustainability of the world's marine fisheries and related habitats.

To achieve this rare honour, the Western Australian fishery has spent the past 37 years implementing a rigorous program of management which has focused on maintaining the lobster

lobster trapping WESTERN AUSTRALIAN FISHING INDUSTRY CO

pristine waters at the mouth of the margaret river, western australia DAVID HAHN AUSTRALIAN WOMEN'S WEEKLY

bster with burnt lemon butter

western rock lobster WESTERN AUSTRALIAN FISHING INDUSTRY COUNCIL

breeding stock and includes such measures as a limited season, minimum size requirement, a ban on catching breeding females, and a strict limit on the number of licensed boats.

The right to carry the Eco-label tag, not easily won, is an indication to consumers all over the world that Australian western rock lobsters are from a sustainable well managed fishery – which means that your great-grandchildren will one day be able to enjoy them as much as you do now.

lamb cutlets in harissa with preserved lemon and olive *couscous*

preparation time 20 minutes ■ cooking time 35 minutes (plus standing time)

CAMEL RACE, BOULIA, QUEENSLAND
Tourism Queensland

8 red Thai chillies, seeded, chopped coarsely
4 cloves garlic, quartered
1 teaspoon salt
2 tablespoons coriander seeds
1 tablespoon cumin seeds
2 teaspoons caraway seeds
1 tablespoon coarsely grated lemon rind
1 tablespoon lemon juice
1/4 cup (60ml) olive oil
2 racks of lamb (6 cutlets each)
1/3 cup (80ml) olive oil, extra
8 saffron threads
2 cups (400g) couscous
20g butter, chopped
2 cups (500ml) boiling water
2 tablespoons finely chopped rinsed preserved lemon
100g cracked green olives, chopped coarsely
1/4 cup fresh mint leaves, shredded finely
1/2 cup (70g) slivered almonds, toasted
200g sheep-milk yogurt

1 Preheat oven to very hot.

2 Blend or process chilli, garlic, salt, seeds, rind, juice and oil until mixture forms harissa paste.

3 Cut slits between cutlets with sharp knife; push one teaspoon of harissa in each slit, press remaining harissa over outside of racks. Place racks in large oiled baking dish; roast, uncovered, in very hot oven about 35 minutes or until browned and cooked as desired. Cover racks; stand 5 minutes before slicing into cutlets.

4 Meanwhile, heat extra oil in small saucepan; stir in saffron. Remove from heat, cool; strain through fine strainer into small jug.

5 Combine couscous, butter and the water in large heatproof bowl; fluff with fork to separate grains. Stir in lemon, olives, mint and almonds. Serve cutlets with couscous and yogurt; drizzle with saffron oil.

SERVES 4

per serving 73.4g fat; 4726kJ

tip Prepared uncooked lamb racks can be made a day ahead and kept, covered, in the refrigerator. Make the harissa up to a month before required; store in a screw-top jar in refrigerator.

Harissa is a fiery spice paste, much used in North African cooking. Here, lamb cutlets are coated in the traditional blend of chillies, cumin and coriander before being baked in a very hot oven, then served with couscous, the perfect accompaniment.

barbecued *filet mignon* with bearnaise butter

preparation time 25 minutes ■ cooking time 30 minutes

125g butter, softened
1 clove garlic, crushed
2 teaspoons finely chopped fresh tarragon leaves
1 teaspoon finely grated lemon rind
1 tablespoon lemon juice
500g piece beef eye fillet
8 slices prosciutto (120g)
4 medium potatoes (800g), cut into wedges
1/4 teaspoon cayenne pepper
1 tablespoon olive oil
400g Swiss brown mushrooms

1 Beat butter, garlic, tarragon, rind and juice in small bowl with electric mixer until well combined; refrigerate bearnaise butter until required.

2 Cut beef into four pieces. Remove and discard rind from prosciutto; wrap two pieces of prosciutto around each piece of beef, securing with toothpicks.

3 Cook beef on heated oiled grill plate (or grill or barbecue) until browned and cooked as desired; cover to keep warm.

4 Meanwhile, boil, steam or microwave potato until just tender; drain, toss in combined pepper and oil.

5 Cook potato and mushrooms on heated oiled grill plate (or grill or barbecue), in batches, until browned.

6 Serve beef topped with a tablespoon of bearnaise butter, and accompanied by potato wedges and mushrooms.

SERVES 4

per serving 41.9g fat; 2640kJ

tip Thin slices of good quality bacon, rind removed, can be used instead of prosciutto.

This recipe substitutes traditional Bearnaise sauce with a tarragon-flavoured butter that melts on top of the steak. Swiss brown mushrooms, also known as portobello, cremini or Roman mushrooms, have a slightly earthier taste than button mushrooms, which could be used instead. We chose red-skinned pontiac potatoes, but just about any other variety could be used.

aussie *meat pie* with pea mash

preparation time 40 minutes (plus refrigeration time)
cooking time 2 hours 10 minutes

HARRY'S CAFE DE WHEELS, WOOLLOOMOOLOO, SYDNEY
Australian Tourist Commission

2 tablespoons olive oil
800g boneless gravy beef, chopped coarsely
1 medium brown onion (150g), chopped finely
2 cloves garlic, crushed
$^{1}/_{4}$ cup (35g) plain flour
$^{1}/_{4}$ cup (60ml) dry red wine
3 cups (750ml) beef stock
2 tablespoons tomato paste
1$^{1}/_{4}$ cups (185g) plain flour, extra
125g cold butter, chopped
2 egg yolks
2 tablespoons iced water

PEA MASH
2$^{1}/_{4}$ cups (350g) shelled peas (1kg unshelled)
2 medium potatoes (400g), chopped coarsely
20g butter

1 Heat half the oil in large saucepan; cook beef, in batches, until browned. Heat remaining oil in same pan; cook onion and garlic, stirring, until onion is soft. Add flour; cook, stirring, 1 minute. Stir in wine, stock and paste; cook, stirring, until mixture boils and thickens. Return beef to pan; simmer, covered, 1$^{3}/_{4}$ hours or until beef is tender. Uncover pan, simmer 10 minutes or until mixture is thickened slightly.

2 Meanwhile, blend or process extra flour and butter until crumbly; add egg yolk and the water, process until ingredients just come together. Knead dough lightly on floured surface until smooth. Wrap pastry in plastic wrap; refrigerate 30 minutes.

3 Preheat oven to hot.

4 Divide pastry into four portions. Roll each portion between sheets of baking paper into rounds large enough to line four 1-cup (250ml) metal pie dishes. Lift pastry into dishes, press into sides, trim edges; place dishes on oven tray. Cover pastry with baking paper, fill with dried beans or rice; bake, uncovered, in hot oven 10 minutes. Remove paper and beans carefully from pastry cases; bake, uncovered, about 10 minutes or until pastry cases are crisp and brown.

5 Just before serving, spoon beef filling into pastry cases; top with pea mash.

pea mash Boil, steam or microwave peas and potato, separately, until tender; drain. Blend or process peas until smooth. Mash potato with butter in large bowl until smooth; stir in peas.

SERVES 4

per serving 57.1g fat; 4695kJ

tip Filling and pastry cases can be made a day ahead. Reheat separately before serving.

"Football, meat pies, kangaroos and Holden cars" runs the popular song listing the Australian national icons. In this recipe, the famous old favourite is given an update with an open pastry case filled with a rich, chunky beef mixture. The pea mash is another traditional touch.

ocean trout in vine leaves with *lentil salad* and braised fennel

preparation time 20 minutes ■ cooking time 25 minutes

3/4 cup (150g) puy lentils
50g butter
1 tablespoon olive oil
2 cloves garlic, crushed
8 baby fennel (1kg), sliced
thickly lengthways
200g vine leaves
4 ocean trout fillets (880g)
1 small red onion (100g), chopped finely
1 cup coarsely chopped fresh
flat-leaf parsley
2 tablespoons olive oil, extra
2 tablespoons lemon juice

1. Cook lentils in large saucepan of boiling water about 20 minutes or until just tender; drain.
2. Meanwhile, melt butter and oil in large saucepan; cook garlic and fennel over low heat, partly covered, about 20 minutes or until fennel is tender, stirring occasionally.
3. Preheat oven to moderate. Rinse vine leaves under cold water; drain. Place six leaves, vein-side up, on board, overlapping edges to form a large circle. Place one piece of fish in the centre of vine-leaf circle; carefully fold leaves over to enclose fish. Place fish parcels in large oiled baking dish; bake in moderate oven 15 minutes.
4. Combine lentils in large bowl with onion, parsley, extra oil and juice.
5. Serve fish on lentil salad with fennel.

SERVES 4

per serving 33.3g fat; 2794kJ

tip Use tweezers to remove bones from fish. If baby fennel is unavailable, use larger bulbs of fennel and cut into thin slices.

Puy lentils are small olive-green lentils from the area around Auvergne in France. They have a distinctive flavour, don't require soaking or sorting, and cook in about half the time of brown lentils, which could still be used in this dish, if you prefer.

Christmas in Australia means many things – the deafening roar of cicadas on a hot blue day, shrieking children in a sparkling pool, cold prawns and hot pudding, and always mangoes – that ambrosial symbol of summer in the Southern Hemisphere.

But only a generation ago, this was not the case: tropical fruit meant bananas and pineapples. A mango seemed impossibly exotic, almost as exotic as the cornucopia of tropical fruits that is available in Australia today. Sapotes, jackfruit, breadfruit, guava, durian, mangosteen, soursop, carambola, pawpaw, rambutan, rollinia, lychee, caimito, abiu, longan – this Who's Who of the tropical fruit world increases every year as more and more varieties are grown with success in the hot, wet, tropical climate of north Queensland and the Northern Territory.

Some are already produced in exportable quantities, others only make it to the southern markets in novelty amounts, but consumer interest is enormous and the exotic fruit industry is set to boom.

So which of these exotic newcomers is which? The popular yellow-skinned carambola, or star fruit, is easy to recognise because of its pretty, star-shaped cross section. The flesh is crisp, juicy and fresh.

Rambutans and lychees, although different, both have leathery red skin (covered in soft hairy spines in the case of rambutans) and a deliciously sweet and juicy white flesh. Also similar in taste, but smoother, browner and more brittle in appearance is the longan.

Sapotes come in black or white varieties, the former known as "chocolate pudding fruit" for its soft, sweet dark-brown flesh, often served with a few drops of vanilla and not completely unlike its namesake.

Soursops, sometimes called prickly custard apples, are large pineapple-shaped fruits with a refreshingly tangy juice, and seeds that are said to be toxic.

Mangosteens, beloved in South-East Asia and considered by many to have the finest taste of all tropical fruit, are round, deep purple fruits containing several white segments with a superb sweet-sour taste.

Fragrant guavas, with their thin yellow-green skin and pinkish fruit, can be eaten raw, poached in a light syrup or used in jams and preserves.

And that still leaves bananas, pineapples, passionfruit, pawpaws, coconuts, mangoes and all the other "old" tropical favourites.

Give them all a taste test, and as for eating them, the simplest rule with most tropical fruits is that it's hard to improve on nature, so don't try – eat them raw and enjoy the sweet taste of paradise.

tropical harvest, darling downs PETER LIK–TOURISM QUEENSLAND

pineapples growing at the foot of the glasshouse mountains, queensland AUSTRALIAN TOURIST COMMISSION

embarrassment of riches

TROPICAL FRUIT

ection of tropical fruit ALAN BENSON

fresh coconut milk
TOURISM QUEENSLAND

desserts

finish with a flourish — a selection inspired by restaurant and cafe menus

coffee-bar *ice-cream*

preparation time 30 minutes (plus standing and freezing time) ■ cooking time 10 minutes

3 cups (750ml) cream
4 egg yolks
1/2 cup (110g) caster sugar
1/4 cup (20g) coarsely ground espresso coffee beans
25g dark chocolate
2 1/2 teaspoons instant coffee powder
120g dark chocolate, melted, extra
2 teaspoons vegetable oil

1 Place cream in medium saucepan; bring to a boil then remove from heat. Remove 1/2 cup of the cream from pan; reserve.

2 Whisk egg yolks and sugar in medium bowl until light and fluffy; gradually whisk in the remaining hot cream. Stand 10 minutes; place equal portions of cream mixture in three small bowls.

3 Combine reserved hot cream with ground coffee; stand 5 minutes. Strain coffee cream into small bowl; discard coffee granules.

4 Make three ice-cream flavours according to instructions below. Pour each variation into a separate 8cm x 26cm bar pan, cover; freeze 3 hours or until just set. Beat ice-creams, separately, in small bowls with electric mixer until smooth. Line base and both long sides of same bar pans with baking paper; return ice-creams to their respective pans. Cover; freeze until firm.

5 Combine extra chocolate with oil, stirring until smooth. Working quickly, spread half of this chocolate mixture evenly over top of frozen latte ice-cream; return latte ice-cream to freezer while assembling the other two ice-creams.

6 Working quickly, spread remaining chocolate mixture over top of frozen mocha ice-cream while still in pan. Turn espresso ice-cream out of bar pan onto serving plate; top with mocha layer, chocolate-top down. Take latte ice-cream from freezer and carefully turn out of bar pan, chocolate-top down, onto mocha layer. Return to freezer until firm. To serve, cut into 1.5cm slices using electric or serrated knife.

latte ice-cream Stir 2 teaspoons of the reserved coffee-cream mixture into one of the bowls containing one-third of the basic ice-cream mixture.

mocha ice-cream Stir dark chocolate, 1/2 teaspoon of the instant coffee powder and two teaspoons of the reserved coffee-cream mixture in small bowl over pan of simmering water until chocolate melts; cool 10 minutes before stirring into a second bowl containing one-third of the basic ice-cream mixture.

espresso ice-cream Dissolve remaining instant coffee with remaining reserved coffee-cream mixture before stirring into remaining bowl of the basic ice-cream mixture.

SERVES 12

per serving 32.9g fat; 1566kJ

tip This ice-cream can be made and assembled up to three days ahead.

Cafe society is alive and well in Australian cities, where the pursuit of the perfect espresso is a popular obsession. Serve this creamy coffee-flavoured confection with thin sweet biscuit wafers, if desired, and decorate with chocolate curls as the ultimate finishing touch.

lemon curd tart with macadamia nut crust

preparation time 25 minutes (plus refrigeration time) ■ cooking time 55 minutes

Long a part of the traditional Aboriginal diet, buttery, sweet macadamia nuts are native to Australia. Used in a pastry crust, the nuts add a delightful hint of crispness to offset the creamy smoothness of the lemon curd.

1/3 cup (50g) macadamias
1 1/4 cups (185g) plain flour
1/3 cup (55g) icing sugar mixture
125g cold butter, chopped
1 egg yolk

LEMON CURD
1 tablespoon finely grated lemon rind
1/2 cup (125ml) lemon juice
5 eggs
3/4 cup (165g) caster sugar
300ml cream

1 Grease a 24cm loose-base flan tin.

2 Process nuts until chopped finely. Add flour, sugar and butter; process until almost combined. Add egg yolk; process until ingredients just come together. Knead dough lightly on floured surface until smooth, cover; refrigerate 30 minutes.

3 Roll pastry between sheets of baking paper until large enough to line prepared tin. Lift pastry into tin; press into side, trim edge. Cover; refrigerate 1 hour.

4 Preheat oven to moderately hot.

5 Cover pastry with baking paper, fill with dried beans or rice, place on oven tray. Bake in moderately hot oven 15 minutes. Remove paper and beans; bake about 10 minutes or until browned lightly, cool.

6 Reduce oven temperature to moderately slow. Pour lemon curd into pastry case, bake in moderately slow oven about 30 minutes or until filling is almost set; cool. Refrigerate until cold.

lemon curd Whisk ingredients in medium bowl; stand 5 minutes.

SERVES 8

per serving 35.7g fat; 2235kJ

tip You need about 3 lemons to make this recipe. You can also use any citrus you like for this tart (finely grated lime rind is a delicious alternative).

serving suggestion Serve tart, dusted lightly with sifted icing sugar mixture, with whole fresh raspberries.

caramelised apples
with almond pastry and maple ice-cream

preparation time 20 minutes ■ cooking time 20 minutes

We used Granny Smith apples here, but you can use other varieties such as Golden Delicious if you prefer.

2 sheets ready-rolled puff pastry
1 egg yolk
1/2 cup (40g) flaked almonds
8 medium apples (1.2kg)
100g butter, chopped
1/2 cup (100g) firmly packed brown sugar
1/3 cup (80ml) orange juice
800g maple-syrup flavoured ice-cream

1. Preheat oven to hot.
2. Cut each pastry sheet into six rectangles; cut four of these rectangles across diagonally to make eight triangles. Brush these triangles with egg yolk; sprinkle with almonds. Place all pastry pieces in single layer on greased oven trays; bake in hot oven 15 minutes or until brown and puffed.
3. Meanwhile, peel and core apples; cut into thin wedges. Melt butter in large frying pan; cook sugar, stirring, until dissolved. Add apple; cook, stirring, until apple begins to caramelise. Add juice; cook, stirring, until apple is just tender.
4. Just before serving, split pastry rectangles in half horizontally. Place one rectangle bottom on each serving plate; top with apple mixture and remaining rectangle half. Top with ice-cream; place single triangles alongside. Dust with sifted icing sugar to serve, if desired.

SERVES 8

per serving 30.1g fat; 2068kJ

tip If you can't find maple-syrup flavoured ice-cream, substitute toffee-crunch or caramel-vanilla flavour instead.

pineapple and mango

in a lime, rum and ginger syrup

preparation time 25 minutes (plus refrigeration time)
cooking time 25 minutes

THE BIG PINEAPPLE, WOOMBYE, QUEENSLAND
Tourism Queensland

2 cups (440g) caster sugar
2 cups (500ml) water
10cm piece fresh ginger, sliced thinly
1/4 cup (60ml) dark rum
1/4 cup (60ml) lime juice
1 large pineapple (2kg)
2 large mangoes (1.2kg)
2 limes

1 Combine sugar, the water and ginger in medium saucepan; stir over heat, without boiling, until sugar dissolves. Bring to a boil; simmer, uncovered, without stirring, about 5 minutes or until syrup has thickened slightly. Stir rum and juice into syrup; cool.

2 Cut pineapple into large, even-size pieces. Slice through mangoes on both sides of seed; score each mango cheek in shallow criss-cross pattern, taking care not to cut through skin.

3 Cook pineapple and mango, in batches, on heated oiled grill plate (or grill or barbecue) until browned all sides. Combine pineapple and mango with syrup in large bowl, cover; refrigerate overnight.

4 Drain fruit over large bowl. Place 2 cups of the syrup in a medium saucepan (discard remaining syrup); bring to a boil. Simmer, uncovered, until syrup is reduced by half. Remove from heat.

5 Using zester, score limes lengthways; slice thickly.

6 Serve pineapple and halved mango cheeks with lime slices; drizzle with syrup.

SERVES 8

per serving 0.4g fat; 1431k

tips Use any pineapple variety you like but discard the hard core before chopping.

Try using other fruits such as star fruit, figs, peaches or bananas.

Pineapple growers in the Glasshouse Mountains in Queensland spent some 10 years developing Bethonga Gold, a hybrid pineapple from Hawaiian stock. Bethonga Gold has no hard core like other pineapples, is sweet year-round and is high in vitamin C.

black label brie THE KING ISLAND COMPANY LTD

a land of milk ...

AUSTRALIAN CHEESE

Ash-coated fresh-curd fromages de chèvre, gooey-hearted brie and camembert, marinated ewe's milk fetta, sweet, fresh buffalo mozzarella, nutty wheels of Swiss-style gruyère, chalky wedges of perfectly matured cheddar, pungent farmhouse blue – because of its size, Australia has a range of seasonal and regional conditions that mean our dairy products are as varied as the landscape itself and in the past 20 years, Australia's specialist cheesemakers have turned the country into a cheeselover's paradise .

Once very much subject to "cultural cringe" when compared with its European counterparts, the Australian cheese industry is now proudly producing high quality products that local consumers continue to embrace with enthusiasm. And, unlike its European peers, Australian cheese enjoys the unique advantage of being produced from animals that are grass-fed year round, rather than spending winter indoors on supplementary feed.

Perhaps the turning point for the industry can be traced to the phenomenal success of The King Island Company. In the mid 1980s, on a tiny windswept island off the north-west tip of Tasmania, the King Island Dairy began to produce and indeed, continues to produce, a range of dairy products that gradually came to convince consumers of just how good Australian dairy foods could be.

Around much the same time, a small number of specialist cheeses started to appear on the market, almost invariably produced by small-scale, farm-based cheesemakers, using traditional and very labour-intensive methods. It was often a labour of love rather than a sound business enterprise, but the result has been the

prime dairy country, bellingen, new south wales AUSTRALIAN TOURIST COMMISSION

brie maturing in cellars THE KING ISLAND COMPANY LTD

gradual re-education of Australian palates and an acceptance of products that not long ago would have sounded totally alien.

Although the favourite national cheese remains cheddar, a growing interest in regional varieties means that of the 11 kilograms of cheese we *each* consume on average every year, five kilograms is now of a non-cheddar variety, reflecting the increasingly diverse nature of our eating habits, as well as the abundant choice of cheeses available in Australia today.

cheesemaker, ueli berger, testing cheese
THE KING ISLAND COMPANY LTD

hot *pavlovas* with frangelico sauce and praline

preparation time 25 minutes ■ cooking time 30 minutes

ESPRESSO AT BAR COLUZZI, DARLINGHURST, SYDNEY
Basquali Skamaachi ATC

3 egg whites
2 cups (320g) icing sugar mixture
1/2 cup (125ml) boiling water
300ml thickened cream

CHOCOLATE FRANGELICO SAUCE
150g dark chocolate, chopped
3/4 cup (180ml) thickened cream
2 tablespoons Frangelico

HAZELNUT PRALINE
2/3 cup (100g) hazelnuts, roasted, chopped
1 cup (220g) caster sugar
1/2 cup (125ml) water

1. Place oven shelves as low as possible in oven; preheat oven to moderate. Grease and line two oven trays with baking paper; trace three 10cm circles about 6cm apart on each tray.
2. Beat egg whites, icing sugar and the water in small bowl with electric mixer about 8 minutes or until soft peaks form. Ladle egg white mixture equally among the six circles.
3. Bake on lowest shelves of moderate oven about 20 minutes or until meringue feels set.
4. Meanwhile, beat cream in small bowl until soft peaks form.
5. Top hot pavlovas with cream, drizzle with chocolate frangelico sauce and sprinkle with crushed hazelnut praline. Decorate with praline shards then serve immediately.

chocolate frangelico sauce Stir chocolate, cream and Frangelico in small saucepan over low heat until chocolate melts; keep warm.

hazelnut praline Place hazelnuts in single layer on a greased oven tray. Combine sugar and the water in small saucepan; stir over heat, without boiling, until sugar dissolves. Bring to a boil; simmer, uncovered, without stirring, until mixture turns a golden brown. Pour over hazelnuts; cool. Break praline into shards; process one-third of the shards until crushed.

SERVES 6

per serving 49.8g fat; 3819kJ

The country of origin for the pavlova is a hotly disputed subject in the Antipodes. Both Australia and New Zealand claim it as their own.

trifle with a twist

preparation time 40 minutes (plus cooling and refrigeration time) ■ cooking time 1 hour

500g (1 1/2 cups) strawberry jam
900ml thickened cream
500g strawberries, halved

LEMON COCONUT SYRUP CAKE
60g butter
2 teaspoons finely grated lemon rind
1/2 cup (110g) caster sugar
2 eggs
1 cup (150g) self-raising flour
1/2 cup (45g) desiccated coconut
1/4 cup (60g) yogurt
1/4 cup (60ml) milk

LEMON SYRUP
1/2 cup (125ml) lemon juice
1/2 cup (110g) caster sugar
1/4 cup (60ml) water

1. Bring jam up to the boil in medium saucepan. Strain jam over small bowl; reserve pulp.
2. Return syrup from jam to saucepan and boil about 5 minutes or until reduced to approximately 3/4 cup.
3. Drizzle about 1 tablespoon of the reduced syrup in zigzag pattern around inside of eight 1-cup (250ml) chilled serving glasses; freeze 30 minutes.
4. Beat two-thirds of the cream in small bowl until soft peaks form. Combine reserved pulp with half of the strawberries in medium bowl. Divide one-third of the whipped cream among the glasses, spreading around inside of glass to cover the jam pattern. Divide half of the strawberry mixture, half of the lemon coconut syrup cake cubes, and half of the remaining whipped cream among glasses; repeat with remaining strawberry mixture, cake and cream. Cover; refrigerate overnight.
5. Just before serving, beat remaining cream in small bowl until soft peaks form. Decorate each trifle with cream and remaining strawberries.

lemon coconut syrup cake Preheat oven to moderate. Grease 8cm x 26cm bar pan; line base and both long sides with baking paper, extending paper 5cm above edges. Beat butter, rind, sugar and eggs in small bowl with electric mixer until light and fluffy (mixture may curdle). Stir in remaining ingredients, in two batches; spread mixture into prepared pan. Bake in moderate oven about 45 minutes. Stand cake in pan 5 minutes; turn onto wire rack over tray. Drizzle hot lemon syrup over hot cake; allow to cool before cutting cake into 2cm cubes.

lemon syrup Combine ingredients in small saucepan; stir over heat, without boiling, until sugar dissolves. Simmer, uncovered, without stirring, 3 minutes; transfer to heatproof jug.

SERVES 8

per serving 53.5g fat; 3883kJ

We've brought the classic trifle into the new century with this spectacular version using lemon coconut syrup cake and served in wine glasses.

caramel and banana
upside-down puddings

preparation time 15 minutes (plus standing time) ■ cooking time 40 minutes

- 2 small overripe bananas (260g), chopped coarsely
- 3/4 cup (180ml) boiling water
- 1/2 teaspoon bicarbonate of soda
- 1 cup (200g) firmly packed brown sugar
- 300ml cream
- 125g butter, chopped
- 60g butter, extra
- 1/2 cup (100g) firmly packed brown sugar, extra
- 2 eggs
- 1 cup (150g) self-raising flour
- 1 cup (100g) coarsely chopped walnuts

1. Preheat oven to moderate. Grease six 1-cup (250ml) metal moulds.
2. Combine banana, the water and soda in small bowl; stand 5 minutes.
3. Meanwhile, combine sugar, cream and butter in medium saucepan; stir over low heat until sugar is dissolved and butter melted. Bring to a boil; simmer 5 minutes or until thickened slightly. Cover caramel sauce to keep hot.
4. Process banana mixture with extra butter and extra sugar until almost smooth; add eggs and flour, process until just combined.
5. Divide nuts among prepared moulds; spoon 2 tablespoons of caramel sauce into each mould. Divide banana mixture among moulds, spooning carefully over caramel to ensure nuts are not dislodged. Bake in moderate oven about 35 minutes. Stand puddings 5 minutes before turning onto serving plates; serve with remaining caramel sauce.

SERVES 6

per serving 60.3g fat; 3580kJ

date *custard tarts*

preparation time 20 minutes (plus refrigeration and standing time) ■ cooking time 45 minutes

$^1/_3$ cup (35g) pecans
$1^1/_2$ cups (225g) plain flour
1 tablespoon caster sugar
125g butter, chopped
1 egg yolk
1 tablespoon milk
9 fresh dates (210g), halved, seeded

CUSTARD FILLING
2 egg yolks
$1^1/_2$ tablespoons caster sugar
1 vanilla bean
$^3/_4$ cup (180ml) cream

1 Grease six 10cm-round loose-base flan tins.

2 Process pecans until finely chopped; add flour, sugar and butter, process until crumbly. Add egg yolk and milk; process until ingredients just come together. Knead dough lightly on floured surface until smooth, cover; refrigerate 1 hour.

3 Preheat oven to moderately hot.

4 Divide pastry into six portions; roll each portion between sheets of baking paper into rounds large enough to line prepared tins. Lift pastry into tins, press into sides, trim edges; place tins on oven tray.

5 Cover pastry with baking paper, fill with dried beans or rice. Bake in moderately hot oven 10 minutes. Remove paper and beans carefully; bake 10 minutes or until browned lightly. Cool.

6 Place three date halves in each pastry case, cut-side-down; pour custard filling into cases, taking care not to dislodge dates. Bake in moderate oven about 25 minutes or until just set (cover with foil halfway during cooking if overbrowning). Serve warm.

custard filling Whisk egg yolks and sugar together in small bowl. Split vanilla bean in half lengthways. Using tip of sharp knife, scrape seeds into bowl with egg mixture; discard pod. Stir in cream; stand 5 minutes.

SERVES 6

per serving 37.5g fat; 2331kJ

passionfruit *panna cotta* with wine syrup and macadamia wafers

preparation time 20 minutes (plus refrigeration time) ■ cooking time 45 minutes

ST KILDA, MELBOURNE, VICTORIA
Adam Bruzzone ATC

You must use canned passionfruit as the fresh fruit does not provide enough liquid.

2 x 170g cans passionfruit in syrup
1/2 cup (110g) caster sugar
2 teaspoons (7g) gelatine
300ml cream
300ml thickened cream
2/3 cup (160ml) sauternes-style dessert wine
1 cup (250ml) water
1/3 cup (80ml) orange juice
1 tablespoon honey

MACADAMIA WAFERS
1 egg white
1/4 cup (55g) caster sugar
2 tablespoons plain flour
30g butter, melted
1/3 cup (50g) macadamia nuts, toasted, chopped finely

1. Grease eight 1/2-cup (125ml) metal moulds, such as darioles. Strain passionfruit over small bowl; reserve syrup, discard seeds.
2. Combine passionfruit syrup and sugar in small saucepan, sprinkle over gelatine; stir over heat, without boiling, until sugar dissolves. Bring to a boil; simmer, uncovered, without stirring, 1 minute. Transfer to medium bowl, stir in cream, cover; cool.
3. Beat thickened cream in small bowl until soft peaks form; fold into passionfruit mixture.
4. Divide mixture among prepared moulds; refrigerate, covered, about 3 hours or until set.
5. Combine wine, the water, juice and honey in small saucepan. Bring to a boil; simmer, uncovered, without stirring, about 15 minutes or until wine syrup reduces by one-third; cool.
6. To serve, turn panna cotta onto serving plates; drizzle with wine syrup, serve with macadamia wafers.

macadamia wafers Preheat oven to moderate. Beat egg white in small bowl with electric mixer until soft peaks form. Gradually add sugar, beating until dissolved between additions; fold in flour and butter. Drop rounded teaspoons of mixture 10cm apart on greased oven trays (allow four per tray). Shape into triangles; sprinkle with nuts. Bake in moderate oven about 5 minutes or until wafers are browned lightly; cool on trays.

SERVES 8

per serving 28.3g fat; 1705kJ

tip Panna cotta can be made ahead and kept, covered, overnight in the refrigerator.

From the Italian for "cooked cream", panna cotta is a smooth, velvety, chilled Italian dessert to which we've added passionfruit pulp and sweet wine for extra richness, and macadamia wafers to complete the journey Down Under.

Many an Australian child will fondly remember the bowl of Christmas nuts that slowly dwindled until only the macadamias were left, not because they weren't absolutely delicious, but because it seemed to require a nuclear explosion to crack them! The average family nutcracker simply wilted at the task, leaving bricks and hammers as the only options for those who refused to give up on the elusive kernel.

Thankfully, to enjoy macadamias these days does not require such enormous effort since they are now marketed in a number of ready-to-eat ways. It should also be added that specific macadamia nutcrackers are also available – stylish affairs, but still obviously based on the principle of the brick and the hammer.

Production of macadamia nuts, the only Australian native plant crop that has been developed commercially as a food, is centred in northern New South Wales and south-eastern Queensland, where the trees thrive in the rich volcanic soil and subtropical, high rainfall climate. On the tall, evergreen trees, spectacular hanging sprays of sweet-scented flowers, called racemes, ripen into clusters of nuts, each one protected by a fibrous green outer husk. The ripe nuts fall to the ground naturally – the tree is not shaken like other nut trees – and are harvested at regular intervals throughout the year. The fat outer husk (that looks rather like a Tahitian lime) is removed on the farm before the more familiar round, brown-shelled nut is transported to a factory for heat-drying, cracking and processing. No bricks and hammers here – the shells are expertly and cleanly removed by powerful blades or rollers.

Macadamia production is one of Australia's largest horticultural industries, with the current value of the Australian crop on the domestic and export market estimated to be about $80 million. There is every reason for the industry to grow. First, the current world production of macadamias only accounts for about 0.5% of the total world trade in tree nuts. Second, and more importantly, as well as tasting delicious, macadamias are a high energy food that turns out to be very good for you as well. Full of protein, they contain no cholesterol, and macadamia oil is between 78% and 84% monounsaturated, which is the highest of any oil, including olive oil. With high amounts of its own antioxidants, it is also the only nut that will stay fresh for long periods without any sign of rancidity.

Australia's indigenous people have always valued the tree they call "kindal kindal" as an important source of delicious and nourishing bush tucker. It's just taken the rest of us a little longer.

macadamias in their fibrous outer husks DAVID YOUNG

macadamia farm, new south wales DAVID YOUNG

one tough nut

MACADAMIAS

shelled macadamias and nutcracker SCOTT CAMERON

recently harvested macadamias AUSTRALIAN HORTICULTURAL CORPORATION

tiramisu

preparation time 40 minutes (plus refrigeration time) ■ cooking time 1 hour

125g butter
2 teaspoons instant coffee powder
3/4 cup (180ml) hot water
100g dark chocolate, chopped
1 cup (220g) caster sugar
3/4 cup (110g) self-raising flour
1/2 cup (75g) plain flour
2 tablespoons cocoa powder
1 egg
1 teaspoon vanilla essence
1 1/2 cups (375ml) water, extra
1/2 cup (110g) caster sugar, extra
1/4 cup (12g) instant coffee powder, extra
2 tablespoons marsala
1 1/2 cups (375g) mascarpone cheese
600ml thick cream
1 tablespoon cocoa powder, extra
200g raspberries

1. Preheat oven to slow. Grease 23cm-square slab cake pan; line base with baking paper.
2. Combine butter, coffee powder, the water, chocolate and sugar in medium saucepan; stir over low heat until chocolate is melted. Place chocolate mixture in large bowl; cool 5 minutes.
3. Whisk in sifted flours and cocoa, in two batches; whisk in egg and essence. Pour into prepared pan; bake in slow oven about 40 minutes. Stand cake 5 minutes; turn onto wire rack to cool.
4. Meanwhile, combine the extra water, extra sugar and extra coffee in medium saucepan; stir over heat, without boiling, until sugar dissolves. Bring to a boil; boil, uncovered, without stirring, 5 minutes. Remove from heat, stir in marsala; cool. Reserve 1/3 cup of this coffee syrup.
5. Split cake in half horizontally; place halves, crust-side up, on flat tray, brush with remaining coffee syrup. Cover; refrigerate 3 hours or overnight.
6. Cut each cake half into eight equal pieces. Combine mascarpone, cream and reserved coffee syrup in medium bowl; whisk gently until mixture thickens slightly.
7. Assemble tiramisu among eight serving dishes: place a piece of cake on each dish, top them all using half of the mascarpone mixture. Repeat, using remaining cake and mascarpone mixture. Dust with extra sifted cocoa; top with raspberries.

SERVES 8

per serving 39.1g fat; 2840kJ

Tiramisu, translated loosely as "pick-me-up", is usually made of savoiardi (lady-finger biscuits), but our version is based on a delectable dark chocolate cake. Mascarpone is a soft, creamy, delicately flavoured cheese that was first introduced to Australian diners in the early 1980s when a single Italian cheesemaker started selling it fresh from his shop in Sydney.

almond berry *friands*

preparation time 15 minutes ■ cooking time 25 minutes

Friands gain their fine texture from the icing sugar and almond meal that partly replace the usual flour. You can use either fresh or frozen berries for this recipe.

185g butter, melted
1 cup (125g) almond meal
6 egg whites, beaten lightly
1½ cups (240g) icing sugar mixture
½ cup (75g) plain flour
35g fresh raspberries
35g fresh blueberries

1 Preheat oven to moderately hot.

2 Grease 12-hole (⅓ cup/80ml) muffin pan.

3 Place butter, almond meal, egg white, icing sugar and flour in medium bowl; stir until just combined.

4 Divide mixture among holes of prepared pan. Scatter the raspberries over six of the pan's holes and the blueberries over the remaining six holes. Bake in moderately hot oven about 25 minutes. Stand friands in pan 5 minutes; turn onto wire rack to cool.

MAKES 12

per friand 18.5g fat; 1182kJ

tip You could also bake these in 12-hole (2 tablespoons/40ml) small muffin pans; this will give you 18 smaller friands.

lamingtons

preparation time 1 hour ■ cooking time 30 minutes

The name of these famous Australian cakes derives from Lord Lamington, a Queensland governor of the late 1800s who always wore a homburg hat, which lamingtons were thought to resemble.

4 eggs
¾ cup (165g) caster sugar
1 cup (150g) self-raising flour
1 tablespoon cornflour
⅓ cup (80ml) boiling water
1 teaspoon butter
2 cups (180g) desiccated coconut, approximately

CHOCOLATE ICING

4 cups (500g) icing sugar mixture
½ cup (50g) cocoa powder
15g butter
⅔ cup (160ml) milk

1 Preheat oven to moderately hot.

2 Grease 20cm x 30cm lamington pan; line base and both long sides with baking paper.

3 Beat eggs in small bowl with electric mixer until thick and creamy; gradually add sugar, beating until dissolved between each addition. Transfer mixture to large bowl.

4 Sift flour and cornflour together three times. Fold triple-sifted flours into egg mixture; stir in combined water and butter. Pour mixture into prepared pan; bake in moderately hot oven about 25 minutes. Turn sponge onto wire rack to cool.

5 Trim crusts on all sides to make an 18cm x 27cm rectangle; cut rectangle into 3cm squares (54 squares in all). Dip squares in chocolate icing; drain off excess, toss squares in coconut. Place lamingtons on wire rack to set.

chocolate icing Combine sifted icing sugar and cocoa in large heatproof bowl; stir in butter and milk. Stir over pan of simmering water until icing is of coating consistency.

MAKES 54

per lamington 3.1g fat; 381kJ

tip Sponge is easier to handle if made a day before making the lamingtons. Fresh cubes of cake can be frozen, then dipped in chocolate icing while frozen.

mini anzac *biscuits*

preparation time 10 minutes ■ cooking time 15 minutes

Anzac biscuits achieved their special place in Aussie hearts during World War I when they were sold at fundraisers to support troops overseas.

40g butter
1 teaspoon golden syrup
1/4 teaspoon bicarbonate of soda
1 tablespoon water
1/4 cup (35g) plain flour
1/4 cup (20g) rolled oats
1/4 cup (20g) desiccated coconut
2 tablespoons caster sugar

1. Preheat oven to moderate.
2. Melt butter with golden syrup in small saucepan over heat; stir in soda and the water.
3. Combine flour, oats, coconut and sugar in small bowl; add butter mixture, stir with wooden spoon until combined.
4. Roll level teaspoons of mixture into balls; place on greased oven trays, allowing 3cm between each biscuit. Press biscuits with fingers to flatten slightly.
5. Bake in moderate oven about 10 minutes. Stand 5 minutes; transfer to a wire rack to cool.

MAKES 25

per biscuit 1.9g fat; 129kJ
tips Biscuits can be kept in an airtight container for up to a week. Re-crisp biscuits by heating on an oven tray in a moderate oven for 5 minutes.

left to right: almond berry friand; mini anzac biscuits; and lamingtons

chocolate *brownies*

preparation time 15 minutes (plus standing time) ■ cooking time 40 minutes

125g butter, chopped
200g dark chocolate, chopped
1/2 cup (110g) caster sugar
2 eggs, beaten lightly
1 1/4 cups (185g) plain flour
100g dark chocolate, chopped, extra
100g milk chocolate, chopped
1/3 cup (35g) pecans, toasted, chopped coarsely

1. Preheat oven to moderate. Grease deep 19cm-square cake pan; line base and sides with baking paper.
2. Combine butter and dark chocolate in medium saucepan; stir over low heat until melted. Cool 10 minutes. Stir in sugar and egg, then flour; add extra dark chocolate, milk chocolate and nuts, stir until ingredients are just combined. Spread mixture into prepared pan.
3. Bake in moderate oven about 35 minutes or until brownie mixture is firm to the touch. Cool brownies in pan before cutting into squares.

MAKES 20

per brownie 12.7g fat; 926kJ

tips Other nuts, such as macadamias or walnuts, can be used in this recipe instead of the pecans.

Dust brownies with sifted icing sugar mixture to serve.

florentines

preparation time 10 minutes (plus standing time) ■ cooking time 15 minutes

60g butter
1/3 cup (75g) firmly packed brown sugar
2 teaspoons golden syrup
2 tablespoons plain flour
1/2 teaspoon ground ginger
1 tablespoon mixed peel
2 tablespoons finely chopped red glacé cherries
1/2 cup (40g) flaked almonds
100g dark chocolate, melted

1. Preheat oven to moderate.
2. Combine butter, sugar and golden syrup in small saucepan; stir over heat, without boiling, until sugar dissolves. Remove from heat. Stir in flour and ginger. Add peel, cherries and nuts; stir to combine.
3. Drop rounded teaspoons of mixture onto greased oven trays, allowing about 6cm between each to allow mixture to spread.
4. Bake in moderate oven about 8 minutes or until golden brown; gently push florentines into shape while still hot. Stand florentines 1 minute before transferring to wire rack to cool.
5. Spread chocolate over flat side of florentines; run a fork through the chocolate before it sets to make a wavy pattern. Stand florentines, chocolate-side up, on wire rack until set.

MAKES 26

per florentine 3.9g fat; 1992kJ

tips To make curved florentines, place over a rolling pin to cool.

Other glacé fruits can be used instead of red glacé cherries: try finely chopped glacé ginger or apricot.

poppy seed and minted orange syrup *muffins*

preparation time 25 minutes (plus standing time) ■ cooking time 40 minutes

1/3 cup (50g) poppy seeds
1/4 cup (60ml) milk
185g softened butter
1 tablespoon finely grated orange rind
1 cup (220g) caster sugar
3 eggs
1 1/2 cups (225g) self-raising flour
1/2 cup (75g) plain flour
1/2 cup (60g) almond meal
1/2 cup (125ml) orange juice

ORANGE SYRUP

1 cup (220g) caster sugar
2/3 cup (160ml) orange juice
1/3 cup (80ml) water
1/4 cup coarsely chopped fresh mint leaves

1. Preheat oven to moderate.
2. Grease 12-hole (1/3 cup/80ml) muffin pan.
3. Combine poppy seeds and milk in small bowl; stand 20 minutes.
4. Meanwhile, beat butter, rind and sugar in medium bowl with electric mixer until light and fluffy; add eggs, 1 at a time, beating until just combined between additions. Stir in flours, almond meal, juice and milk mixture.
5. Divide mixture among holes of prepared pan; bake in moderate oven about 35 minutes. Stand muffins in pan 5 minutes; turn onto wire rack over tray. Drizzle hot syrup over hot muffins.

orange syrup Combine ingredients in small saucepan; stir over heat, without boiling, until sugar dissolves. Simmer, uncovered, without stirring, 2 minutes; transfer to heatproof jug.

MAKES 12

per muffin 18.7g fat; 1750kJ

tip Substitute lemon, lime or mandarin rind and juice for the orange if you prefer another citrus flavour.

left to right: chocolate brownies; florentines; and poppy seed and minted orange syrup muffin

glossary

allspice also known as pimento or Jamaican pepper; available whole or ground. Tastes like a blend of cinnamon, clove and nutmeg.

almonds

BLANCHED skins removed.

FLAKED paper-thin slices.

GROUND also known as almond meal.

SLIVERED small lengthways-cut pieces.

basil

SWEET has a strong, slightly anise-like smell and is an essential ingredient in many Italian dishes.

THAI also known as bai krapow or holy basil; small, crinkly leaves with a strong, somewhat bitter, flavour. Most often used in Asian dishes.

beef

EYE-FILLET tenderloin.

GRAVY shin beef without bone.

SCOTCH FILLET eye of the rib roast; also known as rib-eye.

beetroot also known as red beets or, simply, beets.

bok choy also called pak choi or Chinese white cabbage; has a fresh, mild mustard taste and is good braised or in stir-fries. Baby bok choy is also available.

breadcrumbs

PACKAGED fine-textured, crunchy, purchased, white breadcrumbs.

STALE one- or two-day-old bread made into crumbs by grating by hand, blending or processing.

burghul also known as bulghur wheat; hulled steamed wheat kernels that, once dried, are crushed into various size grains. Used in Middle-Eastern dishes such as tabbouleh.

butter use salted or unsalted ("sweet") butter; 125g is equal to one stick of butter.

buttermilk low-fat milk cultured to give a slightly sour, tangy taste; low-fat yogurt can be substituted.

cannellini (butter) beans small, dried white bean similar in appearance and flavour to other *Phaseolus vulgaris*: great northern, navy and haricot beans.

caperberries fruit formed after the caper buds have flowered; caperberries are pickled.

capers the grey-green buds of a warm climate (usually Mediterranean) shrub sold either dried and salted or pickled in a vinegar brine; used to enhance sauces and dressings.

celeriac tuberous root with brown skin, white flesh and a celery-like flavour. Can be eaten raw or cooked.

cheese

BOCCONCINI small rounds of fresh "baby" mozzarella, a delicate, semi-soft, white cheese traditionally made in Italy from buffalo milk.

BRIE buttery soft cheese with an edible, chalk-like white-mould rind; originally from France but now manufactured locally.

FETTA Greek in origin; a crumbly-textured goat- or sheep-milk cheese with a sharp, salty taste.

FONTINA Italian in origin with a brown or red rind. It is semi-hard with a nutty flavour and a few holes.

GOAT made from goat milk, has an earthy, strong taste; available in both soft and firm textures.

MASCARPONE fresh, thick, triple-cream cheese with a delicately sweet, slightly sour taste.

PECORINO hard, dry, yellow cheese, which has a sharp pungent taste. Originally made from sheep milk, it is now made from cow milk.

RICOTTA sweet, moist, fresh curd cheese having a low fat content.

ROMANO a hard, straw-coloured cheese with a grainy texture and sharp, tangy flavour, usually made from a combination of cow milk and goat- or sheep-milk. A good grating cheese.

chickpeas also called garbanzos, hummus or channa; an irregularly round, sandy-coloured legume used extensively in Mediterranean cooking.

coconut

CREAM available in cans and cartons; made from coconut and water.

MILK pure, unsweetened coconut milk available in cans.

coriander also known as cilantro or Chinese parsley; has bright green leaves and a pungent flavour. The entire plant – roots, stems and leaves – is used in some dishes.

couscous a fine, grain-like cereal product, originally from North Africa; made from semolina.

cream

FRESH (MINIMUM FAT CONTENT 35%) also known as pure cream and pouring cream; contains no additives.

LIGHT SOUR (MINIMUM FAT CONTENT 18%) cream specifically cultured to produce its characteristic tart flavour; thinner than normal sour cream so should not be substituted in cooking because the consistency will affect recipe results.

SOUR (MINIMUM FAT CONTENT 35%) a thick, commercially-cultured soured cream. Good with baked potatoes and for dips, toppings and baked cheesecakes.

CRÈME FRAÎCHE (MINIMUM FAT CONTENT 35%) velvety texture and tangy taste; available in cartons from delicatessens and supermarkets.

cucumber, Lebanese short, slender and thin-skinned, also known as the European or burpless cucumber.

eggplant also known as aubergine.

endive a curly-leafed vegetable, mainly used in salads.

fennel a fresh green bulb also known as finocchio or anise.

fish fillets fish pieces that have been boned and skinned.

fish sauce also called nam pla or nuoc nam; made from pulverised salted fermented fish.

frangelico hazelnut-flavoured liqueur.

galangal a dried root that is a member of the ginger family, used whole or ground, having a piquant peppery flavour. When ground it is usually called laos powder.

garam masala a blend of spices, originating in North India; based on varying proportions of cardamom, cinnamon, cloves, coriander, fennel and cumin, roasted and ground.

gelatine (gelatin) we used powdered gelatine. It is also available in sheet form known as leaf gelatine.

gherkins sometimes known as a cornichons; young cucumbers grown especially for pickling.

ginger

FRESH also known as green or root ginger; the thick gnarled root of a tropical plant.

GLACÉ fresh ginger root preserved in sugar syrup. Crystallised ginger can be substituted if rinsed with warm water and dried before using.

GROUND also known as powdered ginger; used as a flavouring in cakes, pies and puddings but cannot be substituted for fresh ginger.

PICKLED originating from Japan and available in packaged form; thinly shaved ginger pickled in a mixture of vinegar, sugar and natural colouring.

golden syrup a by-product of refined sugarcane; pure maple syrup or honey can be substituted.

green peppercorns soft, unripe berry of the pepper plant usually sold packed in brine (occasionally found dried, packed in salt).

herbs when specified, we used dried (not ground) herbs in the proportion of 1:4 for fresh herbs; eg 1 teaspoon dried herbs equals 4 teaspoons (1 tablespoon) chopped fresh herbs.

hoisin sauce a thick, sweet and spicy Chinese paste made from salted fermented soy beans, onions and garlic; used as a marinade, or to accent stir-fries and barbecued food.

kaffir lime leaves aromatic leaves of a small citrus tree bearing a wrinkled-skinned, yellow-green fruit; used fresh or dried in many Asian dishes.

kangaroo the meat of the Australian native animal is both lean and low in cholesterol. The fillet is the prime cut and requires minimal cooking. Venison or beef could be substituted.

kumara Polynesian name of orange-fleshed sweet potato often confused with yam.

lamb

CUTLET small, tender rib chop.

FRENCH-TRIMMED LAMB SHANKS also known as drumsticks or Frenched shanks; all the gristle and narrow end of the bone is discarded and the remaining meat is trimmed.

MINCED ground lamb.

lavash bread flat, unleavened bread of Mediterranean origin, also called lavoche; rectangular sheets are sold in packets in some supermarkets. Eat straight from the pack or brush with oil, sprinkle with seeds and crisp in the oven.

lemon grass a tall, clumping, lemon-smelling and -tasting, sharp-edged grass; the white lower part of each stem is chopped and used in Asian cooking or for tea.

marsala a sweet fortified wine originally from Sicily.

mesclun a mixture of baby lettuces and other salad leaves, also known as gourmet salad mix; sometimes contains the petals of various flowers.

mint a tangy, aromatic green herb available fresh or dried; of the 30 varieties, pungent peppermint and the milder spearmint are most commonly used in cooking.

mushrooms

CLOUD EAR (WOOD EAR OR DRIED BLACK FUNGUS) swell to about five times their dried size when soaked.

FLAT often misnamed as field mushrooms; large, soft, flat mushrooms with a rich earthy flavour.

OYSTER (ABALONE) grey-white mushrooms shaped like a fan.

SHIITAKE used mainly in Chinese and Japanese cooking; available fresh and dried. Soak dried shiitake in warm water to rehydrate before use.

SWISS BROWN light to dark brown mushrooms with full-bodied flavour; also known as portobello. Button or cup mushrooms can be substituted.

noodles

HOKKIEN also known as stir-fry noodles; fresh wheat flour noodles resembling thick, yellow-brown spaghetti which need no pre-cooking before use.

RICE STICK flat, dried noodles made from rice flour; available thin or wide.

nori dried seaweed; sold in thin sheets, toasted or plain. Used for sushi or as a garnish.

onions

GREEN also known as scallions or (incorrectly) shallots; immature onions picked before the bulbs have formed, having long, bright-green edible stalks.

RED also known as Spanish, or Bermuda onions; sweet-flavoured, large, purple-red onions that are particularly good eaten raw.

SPRING have crisp, narrow, green-leafed tops and large sweet white bulbs; best eaten raw in salads.

palm sugar also known as jaggery or gula jawa; a moulded lump sugar made from distilled palm juice. Available from Asian specialty shops; substitute dark brown sugar.

polenta a flour-like cereal made of ground corn (maize); similar to cornmeal but finer and lighter in colour; also the name of the dish made from it.

preserved lemons a North African specialty; lemons are quartered and preserved in salt and lemon juice.

prosciutto salt-cured, air-dried (unsmoked), pressed ham; usually sold in paper-thin slices, ready to eat.

red curry paste combination of dried red chillies, onions, garlic, oil, lemon rind, shrimp paste, ground cumin, paprika, ground turmeric and ground black pepper.

rice

ARBORIO large, round-grain rice able to absorb a large amount of liquid; especially suitable for risotto.

BASMATI a white, fragrant long-grained rice. It should be washed several times before cooking.

KOSHIHIKARI locally grown rice from the Japanese seed; substitute white, medium-grain rice cooked by the absorption method.

rice paper mostly from Vietnam (banh trang). Made from rice paste and stamped into rounds, with a woven pattern. Dipped momentarily in water, they become pliable wrappers for various Asian spring rolls and savoury fried foods.

sambal oelek (also ulek or olek) Indonesian in origin; a salty paste made from ground chillies.

seeds

BLACK ONION also known as kalonji or nigella, distinctively tangy taste. Used in Indian and Middle-Eastern cooking, and commonly found sprinkled on pide, the Turkish flat bread.

SESAME black and white are the most common seeds, however there are red and brown varieties also.

sesame oil made from roasted, crushed white sesame seeds. Do not use for frying.

shrimp paste also known as trasi and blachan; a strong-scented paste made of salted dried shrimp used in many South-East Asian soups and sauces.

snow peas also called mange tout ("eat all"). Snow pea tendrils are the growing shoots of the plant.

tahini a rich buttery paste made from crushed sesame seeds; used in making hummus and other Middle-Eastern dips and sauces.

tamarind concentrate a thick, purple-black, ready-to-use paste extracted from the pulp of the tamarind bean; it is used as is, with no soaking, stirred into sauces and casseroles.

tofu also known as bean curd, an off-white, custard-like product made from the "milk" of crushed soy beans.

turmeric a member of the ginger family, its root is dried and ground, resulting in the rich yellow powder that gives many Indian dishes their characteristic colour.

vanilla bean dried long, thin pod from a tropical golden orchid grown in South America and Tahiti; the tiny black seeds inside the bean impart a vanilla flavour in baking and desserts.

vietnamese mint not a mint at all, this narrow-leafed, pungent herb, also known as Cambodian mint, daun laksa and laksa leaf, is widely used in South-East Asian soups and salads.

vine leaves we used grapevine leaves sold packaged in brine, either bottled or in cryovac packets.

vinegar

BALSAMIC authentic only from the province of Modena, Italy; made from a regional wine of white Trebbiano grapes specially processed then aged in antique wooden casks to give the exquisite pungent flavour.

RASPBERRY made from fresh raspberries steeped in a white wine vinegar.

RICE WINE also known as seasoned rice vinegar; made from fermented rice and flavoured with sugar and salt.

WHITE made from spirit of cane sugar.

wasabi an Asian horseradish used to make a fiery sauce traditionally served with Japanese raw fish dishes.

wonton wrappers gow gee, egg or spring roll pastry sheets can be substituted to enclose various meat or vegetable fillings.

worcestershire sauce a thin, dark-brown spicy sauce used both as a seasoning and as a condiment.

zucchini also known as courgette, belonging to the squash family. The soft yellow flowers, sometimes with baby vegetables still attached, are available in specialist greengrocers and are used, stuffed with savoury fillings, in Italian cooking.

index

acknowledgements

The publisher would like to thank the following people and organisations for their help in preparing this book:

Jo-Ann Ledger, WA Fishing Industry Council, Cottesloe, Western Australia

Australian Women's Weekly, Sydney, New South Wales

Stella Clark and colleagues, Tourism Queensland, Brisbane, Queensland

Amanda Watkins, Tassal Limited, Hobart, Tasmania

Darling Harbour Authority, Sydney, New South Wales

Helen Waterworth, The King Island Company, Abbotsford, Victoria

Rogaya Alkaff, Australian Horticultural Corporation, Sydney, New South Wales

Ray O'Dell, Consolidated Meat Group, Rockhampton, Queensland

Scott Cameron, McMahons Point, New South Wales

Alan Benson, Sydney, New South Wales

Sweet Land, Harris Park, New South Wales

Toby and Tina Scales, Biloela, Queensland

Lesley Spencer, Oyster Farmers Association, Turramurra, New South Wales

R & IJ Bergan, Quality Butchers, Wahroonga, New South Wales

Isabella Lettini, Parramatta, New South Wales

Deborah Gillespie, Australian Tourist Commission, Woolloomooloo, New South Wales

Martine Guillemin, International Picture Library, Milsons Point, New South Wales

Scott Grimster, Northern Territory Seafood Council, Darwin Northern Territory

Stephen Beckett, Southlight Stock Library, Adelaide, South Australia

John Gunter, Balgowlah, New South Wales

stockists

BISON HOMEWARE
www.bisonhome.com Fax (02) 6273 1126

COUNTRY ROAD HOMEWARES
Enquiries Telephone 1800 801 911
Country Road International Head Office
658 Church Street Richmond, Victoria 3121

DINOSAUR DESIGNS
Telephone (02) 9698 3500
Fax (02) 9698 3533
Email dinosaur@zip.com.au

DOMESTIC POTS
Telephone/Fax 02 9386 4099
252 Bronte Road Waverley, NSW 2024

GIRAFFE GLASS
Telephone (02) 94771151

MOSS RIVER AUSTRALIA
63-73 Ann Street Surry Hills, NSW 2010
Telephone (02) 9211 2151
Fax (02) 9211 22152

MUD AUSTRALIA
(02) 9518 0220 www.mudaustralia.com

SUSIE BARNES GLASS DESIGN
Telephone (02) 9960 1887
Fax (02) 9960 8693

PAGES 6-7: Dinosaur Designs sushi underplate, chopsticks, small dishes, small sushi plate; Susie Barnes Glass Design glass sushi plate; Country Road Homewares wine glasses.
PAGE 8: Dinosaur Designs plates; Country Road Homewares napkin and fork.
PAGE 9: Mud Australia plates; Country Road Homewares knife and placemat.
PAGE 11: Susie Barnes Glass Design platter and sushi plates; Dinosaur Designs shot glasses; Country Road Homewares ottoman and fork.
PAGE 12: Country Road Homewares napkin, cutlery and ottoman; Dinosaur Designs tray; Domestic Pots deep dish by Helen Stephens.
PAGE 13: Mud Australia bowl; Bison Homewares plate; Country Road Homewares napkin, cutlery and tray.
PAGE 15: Dinosaur Designs blue plate; Country Road Homewares white plate and fork; Moss River Australia napkin.
PAGE 18: Mud Australia bowl; Dinosaur Designs small dishes; Country Road Homewares cutlery, table linen and glasses.
PAGE 19: Bison Homewares plates; Moss River Australia linen; Country Road Homewares fork.
PAGE 21: Country Road Homewares napkins, cutlery and table; Susie Barnes Glass Design salad bowl; Giraffe Glass platter and plates.
PAGE 23: Dinosaur Designs small plates, bowls, oval plate and spoons; Country Road Homewares divided antipasto dishes and wine glasses; Moss River Australia napkins.
PAGE 24: Domestic Pots bowls by Jane Sawyer; Mud Australia tray; Dinosaur Designs small dish; Country Road Homewares fork; Moss River Australia cloth.
PAGE 25: Dinosaur Designs underplate and bowl; Country Road Homewares white plate and fork.
PAGE 28: Dinosaur Designs underplate, salad servers and small bowls; Domestic Pots large salad bowl by Peter Rushforth; Moss River Australia tablecloth.
PAGE 29: Bison Homewares plates, beakers and bowls; Country Road Homewares napkins, ottoman and cutlery.
PAGE 30: Domestic Pots bowl by Lex Dickson; Country Road Homewares tray, underplate, napkin and spoon.
PAGE 31: Dinosaur Designs plate; Country Road Homewares bamboo mat, napkin and fork.
PAGE 35: Giraffe Glass platter and plates; Country Road Homewares bamboo mat.
PAGE 37: Mud Australia dinner plates, small tray and pot; Dinosaur Designs salt dish; Country Road Homewares cutlery, underplates and wine glasses; Moss River table linen.
PAGE 39: Dinosaur Designs sushi plates, bowls and chopsticks; Country Road Homewares napkin.
PAGE 40: Giraffe Glass green underplate; Mud Australia square dinner plate; Bison Homewares sauce bottle; Dinosaur Designs salt dish; Moss River Australia napkin and cloth; Country Road Homewares champagne glass.
PAGE 45: Giraffe Glass plates; Dinosaur Designs jug and small dishes; Country Road Homewares glasses, champagne flutes and cutlery; Moss River Australia table linen.
PAGE 47: Susie Barnes Glass Design plates; Country Road Homewares glasses, napkins and cutlery.
PAGE 51: Giraffe Glass blue underplate; Country Road Homewares plate, napkin and cutlery.
PAGE 53: Country Road Homewares basket, plate, glasses, cutlery, linen; Giraffe Glass salt and pepper dish.
PAGE 55: Domestic Pots small pots by Ben Richardson, deep dish by Helen Stephens; Country Road Homewares napkin and cutlery.
PAGE 59: Mud Australia plates and bowls; Country Road Homewares mats and cutlery.
PAGE 61: Country Road Homewares white platter, napkins and ottoman; Dinosaur Designs bowls, plates and spoons.
PAGE 65: Domestic Pots deep dish by Helen Stephens, bowls and cups by Jane Sawyer; Dinosaur Designs jug and spoon; Country Road Homewares linen and fork.
PAGE 67: Susie Barnes Glass Design platter, plate and bowl; Country Road Homewares spoon and ottoman.
PAGE 69: Bison Homewares underplates; Mud Australia dinner plates; Moss River Australia table linen; Country Road Homewares glasses.
PAGE 71: Domestic Pots bottles and wine cups by Robert Barron; Country Road Homewares plate and napkin.
PAGE 75: Mud Australia dinner plate and square platter; Country Road Homewares glasses and underplate; Moss River Australia table linen; Dinosaur Designs small dishes.
PAGE 77: Country Road Homewares ottoman, placemat, white plate, glass and napkin; Mud Australia green plate.
PAGE 81: Dinosaur Designs green plates, bowl and spoon; Country Road Homewares white plates, cutlery, table linen and glasses.
PAGE 83: Bison Homewares dinner plate; Mud Australia underplate; Country Road Homewares napkins, linen, glasses and cutlery.
PAGE 85: Country Road Homewares linen, plates, glasses, cutlery.
Page 87: Bison Homewares plates; Dinosaur Designs spoon and bowls; Country Road Homewares napkin and fork.
PAGES 88-89: Country Road Homewares table, white-footed platter and basket.
PAGE 91: Country Road Homewares plates, cutlery, linen, glasses.
PAGE 92: Domestic Pots square celadon plate by Geoff Crispin; Country Road Homewares napkin and fork.
PAGE 93: Giraffe Glass plates; Country Road Homewares spoon and napkin.
PAGE 95: Susie Barnes Glass Design plates; Dinosaur Designs bowl; Country Road Homewares cutlery and napkin.
PAGE 99: Country Road Homewares plates, cutlery and linen.
PAGE 101: Country Road Homewares glasses, table linen and spoon; Giraffe Glass plates.
PAGE 102: Mud Australia plates and small pots; Country Road Homewares spoon.
PAGE 103: Susie Barnes Glass Design plates; Country Road Homewares napkins, cup, saucer and fork.
PAGE 104: Mud Australia pink plate; Country Road Homewares white plate, napkins and cutlery; Giraffe Glass small square plates; Bison Homewares beakers.
PAGE 109: Susie Barnes Glass Design plates; Dinosaur Designs tray; Country Road Homewares table linen and glasses.
PAGE 111: Dinosaur Designs spoon, orange plate, saucer and bowl; Mud Australia underplates; Country Road Homewares cup.
PAGE 113: Domestic Pots cups and saucers by Anthony Brink and square dish by Simon Reece; Susie Barnes Glass Design platter; Country Road Homewares table, napkins and fork; Moss River Australia table mat.

facts and figures

Wherever you live, you'll be able to use our recipes with the help of these easy-to-follow conversions. While these conversions are approximate only, the difference between an exact and the approximate conversion of various liquid and dry measures is but minimal and will not affect your cooking results.

dry measures

metric	imperial
15g	1/2oz
30g	1oz
60g	2oz
90g	3oz
125g	4oz (1/4lb)
155g	5oz
185g	6oz
220g	7oz
250g	8oz (1/2lb)
280g	9oz
315g	10oz
345g	11oz
375g	12oz (3/4lb)
410g	13oz
440g	14oz
470g	15oz
500g	16oz (1lb)
750g	24oz (1 1/2lb)
1kg	32oz (2lb)

liquid measures

metric	imperial
30ml	1 fluid oz
60ml	2 fluid oz
100ml	3 fluid oz
125ml	4 fluid oz
150ml	5 fluid oz (1/4 pint/1 gill)
190ml	6 fluid oz
250ml	8 fluid oz
300ml	10 fluid oz (1/2 pint)
500ml	16 fluid oz
600ml	20 fluid oz (1 pint)
1000ml (1 litre)	1 3/4 pints

helpful measures

metric	imperial
3mm	1/8in
6mm	1/4in
1cm	1/2in
2cm	3/4in
2.5cm	1in
5cm	2in
6cm	2 1/2in
8cm	3in
10cm	4in
13cm	5in
15cm	6in
18cm	7in
20cm	8in
23cm	9in
25cm	10in
28cm	11in
30cm	12in (1ft)

oven temperatures

These oven temperatures are only a guide. Always check the manufacturer's manual.

	°C (Celsius)	°F (Fahrenheit)	Gas Mark
Very slow	120	250	1
Slow	150	300	2
Moderately slow	160	325	3
Moderate	180 - 190	350 - 375	4
Moderately hot	200 - 210	400 - 425	5
Hot	220 - 230	450 - 475	6
Very hot	240 - 250	500 - 525	7

helpful measures

The difference between one country's measuring cups and another's is, at most, within a 2 or 3 teaspoon variance. (For the record, 1 Australian metric measuring cup holds approximately 250ml.) The most accurate way of measuring dry ingredients is to weigh them. When measuring liquids, use a clear glass or plastic jug with the metric markings. (One Australian metric tablespoon holds 20ml; one Australian metric teaspoon holds 5ml.)

If you would like to purchase *The Australian Women's Weekly* Test Kitchen's metric measuring cups and spoons (as approved by Standards Australia), turn to page 120 for details and order coupon. You will receive:

- a graduated set of 4 cups for measuring dry ingredients, with sizes marked on the cups.
- a graduated set of 4 spoons for measuring dry and liquid ingredients, with amounts marked on the spoons.

Note: North America, NZ and the UK use 15ml tablespoons. All cup and spoon measurements are level.

We use large eggs having an average weight of 60g.

how to measure

When using graduated metric measuring cups, shake dry ingredients loosely into the appropriate cup. Do not tap the cup on a bench or tightly pack the ingredients unless directed to do so. Level top of measuring cups and measuring spoons with a knife. When measuring liquids, place a clear glass or plastic jug with metric markings on a flat surface to check accuracy at eye level.